my revision notes

Edexcel AS and A-level History

RUSSIA IN REVOLUTION

1894–1924

Robin Bunce

D1585579

HODDER
EDUCATION
AN HACHETTE UK COMPANY

Orders: please contact Bookpoint Ltd, 130 Milton Park, Abingdon, Oxon OX14 4SE. Telephone: +44 (0)1235 827720. Fax: +44 (0)1235 400454. Email education@bookpoint.co.uk Lines are open from 9 a.m. to 5 p.m., Monday to Saturday, with a 24-hour message answering service. You can also order through our website: www.hoddereducation.co.uk

ISBN: 978 1 4718 7658 5

© Robin Bunce 2017

First published in 2017 by

Hodder Education,

An Hachette UK Company

Carmelite House

50 Victoria Embankment

London EC4Y 0DZ

www.hoddereducation.co.uk

Impression number   10 9 8 7 6 5 4 3 2

Year   2021 2020 2019 2018 2017

Cover photo © Rinat Maksutov/123RF.com

Illustrations by Integra

Typeset by Integra Software Services Pvt. Ltd., Pondicherry, India

Printed in India

A catalogue record for this title is available from the British Library.

My revision planner

REVISED

5   Introduction

1: The rule of Nicholas II, 1894–1905

6   The nature of autocratic rule: the Tsarist principles of autocracy, nationality and Orthodoxy
8   The nature of autocratic rule: Orthodoxy, anti-Semitism and the Okhrana
10   Opposition to Tsarism
12   Opposition to Tsarism: Social Democrats and the Socialist Revolutionaries
14   The 1905 Revolution
16   The 1905 Revolution: the spread of revolutionary activity
18   Nicholas II's response
20   The recovery of Tsarist power
22   Exam focus (AS Level)

2: The end of Romanov rule, 1906–17

26   Change and continuity in government
28   Nicholas II's relations with the Dumas, 1906–14
30   Stolypin's repression, 1906–14
32   Stolypin's reforms, 1906–14
34   The last years of peace
36   The impact of the First World War
38   The impact of the First World War: political problems
40   The February Revolution
42   The Provisional Committee and the Petrograd Soviet
44   Exam focus

3: The Provisional Government and its opponents, February–October 1917

46   The nature of dual power
48   The aims and membership of the Petrograd Soviet
50   Opposition to the Provisional Government
52   Opposition to the Provisional Government, April to July
54   The second Provisional Government, July–October
56   Economic and political problems
58   The October Revolution
60   The events of 24–26 October and the formation of the Bolshevik government
62   Exam focus (AS Level)

4: Defending the Bolshevik revolution, October 1917–24

66 Consolidating Bolshevik power
68 The Cheka and the Red Terror
70 Bolshevik economic policies
72 The crisis of 1921
74 Civil War
76 Defeat of domestic enemies
78 Foreign intervention in Russia
80 Exam focus

81 **Glossary**
83 **Key figures**
85 **Answers**
87 **Mark scheme**

REVISED

Introduction

About Paper 2

Paper 2 Option 2C.2: Russia in revolution, 1894–1924, is a depth study. Therefore it requires a detailed knowledge of the period that you are studying. Paper 2 tests you against two Assessment Objectives: AO1 and AO2.

AO1 tests your ability to:
- organise and communicate your own knowledge
- analyse and evaluate key features of the past
- make supported judgements
- deal with concepts of cause, consequence, change, continuity, similarity, difference and significance.

On Paper 2, AO1 tasks require you to write an essay from your own knowledge.

AO2 tests your ability to:
- analyse and evaluate source material from the past
- explore the value of source material by considering its historical context.

On Paper 2, the AO2 task requires you to write an essay which analyses two sources from the period you have studied.

At A-level, Paper 2 is worth 20 per cent of your qualification. At AS Level, Paper 2 is worth 40 per cent of your qualification. Significantly, your AS grade does not count towards your overall A-level grade. Therefore, you will have to take this paper at A-level in order to get the A-level qualification.

Structure

At AS and A-level, Paper 2 is structured around four key topics which cover the period 1894–1924. The AS and A-level exams are divided into two sections. Section A tests your source analysis skills, whereas Section B tests your ability to write an essay from your own knowledge. Both sections focus on the four key topics. The question may deal with aspects of one of the topics, or may be set on issues that require knowledge of several or all of the topics.

Aspect of the course	AO	Exam
Key Topic 1: The rule of Nicholas II, 1894–1905		
Key Topic 2: The end of Romanov rule, 1906–17	AO1 & AO2	Section A and Section B
Key Topic 3: The Provisional Government and its opponents, February–October 1917		
Key Topic 4: Defending the Bolshevik revolution, October 1917–24		

The exam

At AS and A-level, the Paper 2 exam lasts for 1 hour and 30 minutes. It is divided into two sections, both of which test the depth of your historical knowledge. Section A requires you to answer one compulsory question on two sources. Section B requires you to write one essay. As this is a depth paper, questions can be set on single events or programmes but may cover more extended periods.

How to use this book

This book has been designed to help you to develop the knowledge and skills necessary to succeed in the exam. The book is divided into four sections – one for each of the key topics. Each section is made up of a series of topics organised into double-page spreads. On the left-hand page, you will find a summary of the key content you need to learn. Words in bold in the key content are defined in the glossary. On the right-hand page, you will find exam-focused activities. Together, these two strands of the book will take you through the knowledge and skills essential for exam success.

There are three levels of exam-focused activities:
- Band 1 activities are designed to develop the foundational skills needed to pass the exam.
- Band 2 activities are designed to build on the skills developed in Band 1 activities and to help you achieve a C grade.
- Band 3 activities are designed to enable you to access the highest grades.

Some of the activities have answers or suggested answers on pages 85–86.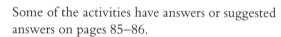

Each section ends with an exam-style question and model high-level answer with commentary. This should give you guidance on what is required to achieve the top grades.

1 The rule of Nicholas II, 1894–1905

The nature of autocratic rule: the Tsarist principles of autocracy, nationality and Orthodoxy

Nicholas II became Tsar of the **Russian Empire** in 1894. He ruled as an autocrat: the sole and absolute ruler of Russia. Nicholas II's rule was particularly **reactionary** and oppressive.

Autocracy

Nicholas II had total power within the Russian Empire. The Tsar was assisted by the **cabinet**, the **Senate** and the **State Council**. However, these bodies were merely advisory; having no power independent of the Tsar.

The Tsar and the law

The Tsar's power was not constrained by any **constitutional checks**. Therefore:
- the Tsar's power was not limited by law
- Russian **subjects** had no right to free speech or a fair trial because these rights would effectively limit the Tsar's power.

The consequences of autocracy

Autocracy led to the development of a corrupt government, and a society that depended on the state.

Corruption

Corruption was widespread because government officials claimed to be representatives of the Tsar, and therefore acted as if they had absolute power.

Limited civil society

Tsarist autocracy also limited the growth of **civil society**. Nicholas II's government outlawed some groups such as trades unions, and persecuted religious groups which could have played a role in generating civil society.

The Tsar's isolation

The Tsar refused to recognise Russia's problems, and his advisers were unwilling to contradict him. As a result, the Tsar had little understanding of the poverty in Russia, or of the government's corruption.

Nationalism and Russification

Between 1894 and 1905 Nicholas II used **Russification** to control the Russian Empire. Russification meant the aggressive promotion of Russian culture and the forceful suppression of other national cultures.

Russification was a response to the development of **nationalist** feeling in various parts of the Empire, which the Tsar believed threatened the unity of the Empire. Indeed, in the late nineteenth century there had been considerable growth of nationalism in the Ukraine, Finland, Georgia and Poland. Russification took a variety of forms:
- The imposition of Russian as the official language of government and the justice system in the government of the **Baltic states**.
- The promotion of Russian culture through primary schools.
- The suppression of non-Russian cultures.
- Establishing Russian-language universities such as Iur'ev University in Estonia.

The consequences of Russification

Russification was counterproductive. It led to a backlash among groups who had been loyal to the Empire. Indeed, cultural persecution turned the Finns, the Armenians and the people of the Baltic against the Tsar:
- The nationalism in Poland and the Baltic states became a powerful anti-government force, which would later feed into the **1905 Revolution**.
- In Russia, nationalism led to anti-Polish, anti-Finnish and anti-Semitic feeling, which sometimes led to violence against minority communities living in Russia.

Russification in Finland

Russification had a major impact on Finland. In 1899 General Nicholas Bobrikov, the governor general of Finland, abolished the Finnish legal system and replaced it with Russian law. He also effectively abolished the Finnish parliament and the Finnish army.

In 1903 '**Temporary Regulations**', which had been introduced in 1881 in Russia, were extended to Finland, giving the **Okhrana** wide-ranging powers (see page 8). The result was widespread unrest. Bobrikov was assassinated in 1904 and the Finns played an active part in the 1905 Revolution.

Support or challenge?

Below is a sample exam question which asks how far you agree with a specific statement. Below this are general statements which are relevant to the question. Using your own knowledge and the information on the opposite page, decide whether these statements support or challenge the statement in the question and circle the appropriate response.

'The fundamental problems with autocracy were the main reason for the collapse of Tsarism in the period 1894–1917.' How far do you agree with this statement?

	Support	Challenge
Autocracy led to widespread corruption.		
The government of Russia was based on the sole authority of the Tsar.		
The Tsar's subjects did not have legally defensible rights.		
The Tsar's advisers argued that autocracy saved the people of Russia from living godless lives.		
There was an increasing gap between the people and the Tsar under Nicholas II.		

 Identify the concept a

Look at the six sample exam questions based on some of the following concepts:
- Cause – questions concern the reasons for something, or why something happened.
- Consequence – questions concern the impact of an event, an action or a policy.
- Change/continuity – questions ask you to investigate the extent to which things changed or stayed the same.
- Similarity/difference – questions ask you to investigate the extent to which two events, actions or policies were similar.
- Significance – questions concern the importance of an event, an action or a policy.

Read each of the questions and work out which of the concepts they are based on.

1 'The fundamental problems with autocracy were the main reason for the collapse of Tsarism in the period 1894–1917.' How far do you agree with this statement?

2 How far did Tsarist rule change in the period 1894–1905? **AS**

3 How accurate is it to say that Nicholas II's rule was fundamentally unstable in the years 1894–1905?

4 How far do you agree that Russification was responsible for the political stability of Russia in the years 1894–1904? **AS**

5 How far was political unrest the most important consequence of Nicholas II's autocratic rule in the period 1894–1905?

6 'Nicholas II's policies fundamentally undermined autocratic rule in the period 1894–1914.' How far do you agree with this view?

The nature of autocratic rule: Orthodoxy, anti-Semitism and the Okhrana

Tsarism relied on **Orthodoxy**, anti-Semitism and the Okhrana, as well as Russification to control the Russian people.

Promoting Orthodoxy

Konstantin Pobedonostsev advised the Tsar to promote Orthodoxy as an essential part of Russian identity. Consequently, between 1894 and 1902 Nicholas introduced the following measures:

● The number of parish clergy increased by around 60 per cent.
● There was a tenfold increase in church schools, and the number of students they educated increased around 15 times.
● Orthodox missionaries were sent to establish new churches in the Baltic states where Protestantism was popular.

As a result the number of people converting to Orthodoxy doubled in the period 1881 to 1902. Nonetheless, in urban areas, there was a decline in Orthodox Church attendance.

Persecuting other faiths

Nicholas II also persecuted other faiths:
● No Christian Churches other than the Orthodox Church were allowed to **proselytise**.
● Catholic, Protestant and Islamic schools were closed down and replaced by schools run by the Russian government.
● The Russian government confiscated the property of the Armenian Church.

Anti-Semitism

Aggressive Russification and the promotion of Orthodoxy led to increased anti-Semitism.

Education

Educational opportunities for Jewish students were limited by the enforcement of quotas. Jews could make up no more than:
● ten per cent of students at universities within the **Pale of Jewish Settlement**
● three per cent in Russia's major cities, Moscow and St Petersburg.

Residency

There were also restrictions on where Jews could live. The May Laws, introduced in 1882, banned Jews from living in Russia's rural areas – the law was finally repealed in 1905.

In some cities, such as Moscow and Kiev, campaigns were organised to expel Jews from cities.

Violence

Under Nicholas II the number of **pogroms** increased dramatically. Indeed in 1903 and 1904 there were 49 pogroms in Russia.

Emigration

Due to growing violent anti-Semitism large numbers of Jews left Russia. Most went to the US but a significant minority headed for Latin America, particularly Argentina and Peru. The government viewed emigration as a good solution to the 'Jewish problem'.

The Okhrana

The Okhrana had a reputation for being 'all-powerful, all-knowing and all-capable'. Its goal was to destroy subversive organisations. In order to do this it had extensive powers to arrest and infiltrate opposition groups.

In reality the Okhrana was relatively small, consisting of around 2,500 agents in 1900. However, it was effective, and before 1905 it had infiltrated the leadership of the Social Democrats and the Socialist Revolutionaries (see page 12).

Sergei Zubatov

Sergei Zubatov became head of the Moscow Okhrana in 1896. In addition to repression, Zubatov introduced 'Police Socialism'. Consequently, the Okhrana:
● investigated workers' complaints about abuses in factories
● attempted to take control of emerging unions
● provided sick pay and unemployment benefit.

Zubatov's experiment spread to other Russian cities. However, the government ended the policy and sacked Zubatov in 1903.

University life

The Okhrana were also involved in policing Russia's universities. The University Statute of 1884:
● banned clubs and societies on university campuses
● emphasised that students should study traditional subjects
● banned women from higher education.

Surveillance

The Okhrana was engaged in widespread surveillance. By 1900 they had records on 55,000 people, collections of 5,000 publications by revolutionary groups and 20,000 photographs of suspected radicals.

Select the detail

Below is a sample A-level exam question with the accompanying sources. Having read the question and the sources, complete the following activity.

> How far could the historian make use of Sources 1 and 2 together to investigate the role of the Okhrana in the period 1894–1905? Explain your answer, using both sources, the information given about them and your own knowledge of the historical context.

Consider the following three claims that you could make when answering the question. Read the claims and then select quotes from the sources to support them.

Remember to keep the quotes short, never copy more than a sentence.

1 Both sources are useful because they contain evidence that the Okhrana was involved in surveillance.

2 Source 2 is useful because it gives a detailed account of the work of Okhrana agents.

3 The two sources are valuable to a historian because they give radically different perspectives on the work of the Okhrana.

SOURCE 1

From the memoirs of A.T. Vassilyev, last Tsarist chief of police. His book, entitled *The Okhrana,* was published in the 1930s.

Much that was mysterious, enigmatical, and dreadful was associated in the mind of the Russian people with the term Police Department. For great sections of the population this office signified frankly a phantom of terror, of which the most improbable tales were told. Many people seriously believed that in the Police Department the unhappy victims of the Okhrana were dropped through a hole in the floor into the cellar, and there tortured.

SOURCE 2

From Victor Serge's book *What Everyone Should Know About State Repression,* published in 1926. Serge was an anarchist in his youth but joined the Bolsheviks in 1919.

In Russia, 'secret agents' – who in fact were spies and provocateurs – belonged to the Okhrana. Its many agents, who were paid 50 roubles a month, had only one job: to spy on the person they were assigned to, hour after hour, day after day, with no interruption.

Daily reports were sent to the police to be analysed by specialists. These officers were dangerously perceptive. They would draw up tables showing a person's actions, the number of visits, their length, regularity, etc. Sometimes, these tables brought out the importance of one member's relationships and his probable influence.

The police chief Zubatov – who tried to gain control of the workers' movement, by setting up his own unions in them – brought this system of espionage to its highest level of perfection. His special brigades could follow a man throughout Russia, even throughout Europe, moving with him from one city to the next, from one country to the next.

The Okhrana had the special mission of seeking out and placing under constant watch those revolutionaries considered the most dangerous, mainly terrorists or members of the Socialist Revolutionary Party who practised terrorism.

Opposition to Tsarism

Worker and peasant opposition to the Tsar was mainly due to the harshness of conditions in Russia. Middle-class opponents of Tsarism, by contrast, wanted political reforms.

Peasant life

The peasants made up 80 per cent of the Russian population in 1894. The vast majority of Russia's peasants lived an impoverished life of hard work, large debt and high taxes. Moreover, most Russian peasants owned little or no land.

Fearing peasant discontent, Nicholas II introduced a series of counter-reforms. These took away freedoms that Russian peasants had enjoyed since the 1860s, thus causing resentment among the peasants:
- Land Captains replaced zemstvos (committees elected by local people) as the key authority in local government. Land Captains managed the work of peasants, and administered law and order.
- Peasants lost the right to elect people to the local zemstvos. Land Captains made the final decision regarding which candidates were allowed to serve on the zemstvos.

The working class

Russia's urban factory workers made up about four per cent of the population in 1894. The working class emerged as a result of **Sergei Witte**'s attempt to industrialise the economy in the 1890s. Witte was one of the Tsar's most trusted and talented ministers, who oversaw the early stages of Russia's industrialisation.

Russia's workers were better paid than the peasants. However, factories were dangerous. Additionally, living conditions in the large slums of Vyborg, Shuliavka and Nakhalovka, in the Empire's major cities, were squalid. Consequently, the mortality rate of workers was higher than the mortality rate of the peasants.

Working conditions were extremely tough. The majority of workers were expected to work a 12-hour day, although some were forced to work up to 17 hours a day. Factory managers could beat their employees and subject them to verbal abuse and degrading body searches.

Harsh conditions and obvious inequalities led to strikes and to the growth of **socialist** groups in Russia's cities.

The League of Liberation

In 1903 middle-class opponents of autocracy formed the League of Liberation. The League was led by **Pavel Milyukov** and **Pyotr Struve**.

Russia's **bourgeoisie**, which made up around 1.5 per cent of the population in 1894, tended to want to democratise Russia. Middle-class demands tended to be **reformist** or **liberal**. Generally, many politically active members of the middle class wanted:
- a government in which elected representatives of the Russian people made laws
- a government that respected individual rights.

The League's demands

The newly formed League published a programme in early 1904, following its first Congress, which was held in St Petersburg. The programme put forward political, social and economic demands, including:
- an end to autocracy
- democratic government based on **universal suffrage**
- a maximum eight-hour day for workers
- redistribution of land to the peasants
- **self-determination** for all nations that were part of the Russian Empire.

The composition of the League

The League of Liberation represented two groups. The League represented the ideas of urban middle-class intellectuals and people who held elected positions in the zemstvos. In this sense the League represented liberal opinion in the country and the cities.

Conflict with the government

The government believed that the League was dangerous. Therefore, the Okhrana arrested leading members of the League soon after its first Congress.

Add the context

Below are sample AS and A-level exam questions with the accompanying sources. Having read the question and the sources, complete the following activity.

Why is Source 1 valuable to the historian for an enquiry into the goals of Russian liberals in the years 1900–04? Explain your answer using the source, the information given about it and your own knowledge of the historical context. **AS**

How far could the historian make use of Sources 1 and 2 together to investigate the goals of the League of Liberation in the years 1903–05?

First, look for aspects of the source that refer to the events and discussion that were going on around the time that the source was written. Underline the key phrases and write a brief description of the context in the margin next to the source. Draw an arrow from the key phrase to the context. Try to find three key phrases in each source. Tip: look at the information above the source – you should contextualise this too. Pay particular attention to the date on which the source was written.

SOURCE 1

From the Programme of the League of Liberation, issued at the League's First Congress held in January 1904 in St Petersburg.

The first aim of the League of Liberation is the political liberation of Russia. Political liberty in even its most minimal form is completely incompatible with the autocracy of the Russian monarchy. Therefore, the Union will seek before all else the abolition of autocracy and the establishment in Russia of a constitutional regime.

In determining the specific forms of a constitutional regime in Russia, the League of Liberation will make all efforts to have political problems solved in the spirit of extensive democracy. Above all, the League recognises as fundamentally essential that the principles of universal and equal suffrage, direct elections, and secret ballot be made the basis of political reform.

Putting political demands at the forefront, the League of Liberation recognises as essential the need to address social and economic problems. In terms of social and economic policy the League will follow the principle of democracy and defend the interests of the toiling masses.

Regarding the national question the League recognises the right to self-determination. In relation to Finland the League supports for the restoration of the constitution which existed in the country before it was illegally changed by the current Tsar.

SOURCE 2

From an article by Pyotr Struve published in the first edition of *Liberation* in July 1903. Struve was living in exile in Germany at the time he wrote the essay. Nonetheless, *Liberation* was distributed illegally in Russia in the period 1903–05.

Social-democratic principles have irresistible power because they are the demands of common morality and justice. These principles are identical with the pure ideas of liberalism: a political system of freedom and equality. Hence, a liberalism which opposes social-democracy opposes its own principles, in favour of supporting privilege.

Any form of liberalism which does not put forward clear and bold political and social-democratic demands will fail to defend the interests of social progress. Hence, no important stream of the Russian Liberation League can ignore the needs of workers and peasants. The League has to include courageously in its programme demands for serious social reform to the advantage of the peasants and the workers. It is not too late for Russian liberals to adopt the correct political position – not against but alongside and united with social-democracy.

Opposition to Tsarism: Social Democrats and the Socialist Revolutionaries

REVISED

In addition to Russian liberals, the Tsar also faced socialist opponents. Between 1898 and 1902 two major socialist parties were formed.

The Social Democrats

The Marxist Russian Social Democratic Labour Party (RSDLP) were established in 1898.

Marxism

Marxism emerged as a movement in the late nineteenth century. Inspired by **Karl Marx**, Marxists argued that industrialisation and capitalism led to the exploitation of the **proletariat**. They advocated a proletarian revolution against capitalism to create a genuinely free and equal society.

Divisions in the RSDLP

Russian Marxists disagreed fundamentally on the strategy of the RSDLP:

- **Lenin** and the **Bolsheviks** argued that the proletariat in Russia was too weak and poorly educated to create a revolution. Therefore they argued that the RSDLP should become a vanguard party: a small secretive party of professional revolutionaries who would lead a revolution on behalf of the workers.
- Julius Martov, Fyodor Dan and the **Mensheviks** argued that the RSDLP should be a mass party which educated and organised the proletariat.

The Socialist Revolutionaries (SRs)

Founded in 1902, the Socialist Revolutionaries stressed the needs of Russia's peasants. The SRs' main aim was **land reform**. They also believed that peasant communes (or *mirs*) could become the basis of a new socialist society.

Viktor Chernov, the leading figure in the SRs, was influenced by Marxism, and argued that together the proletariat and the peasants should overthrow the Tsar.

Political violence

Some SRs, influenced by **anarchism** and **nihilism**, stressed the importance of revolutionary violence. Radical SRs and populists were responsible for the assassination of:

- Nikolay Bogolepov – the Tsar's Education Minister, in 1901
- Vyacheslav von Plehve – the Minister of the Interior, in 1904.

Reasons for the failure of opposition groups

Opposition groups faced a series of obstacles. Consequently, the SRs and the RSDLP remained small, with no more than 100,000 members between them by 1905.

Divisions

Opposition to the Tsar was profoundly divided:

- Liberals wanted reforms to guarantee political rights, whereas socialists wanted a full-scale revolution to change the economic and social structure of Russia.
- The RSDLP was divided between Bolsheviks and Mensheviks. The SRs were divided on the issue of violence.

Repression

The government were extremely successful at neutralising opposition groups through various forms of oppression:

- The Okhrana exiled leading radicals.
- Lenin was exiled to Siberia.
- Pavel Milyukov and Pyotr Struve were both banned from attending the first Congress of the League for Liberation.

Strike breaking

The police and army used extreme violence to end strikes on almost 800 occasions between 1900 and 1902.

The *ukase*

In order to defuse political opposition, the Tsar issued a decree or *ukase* in December 1904 stating that the government would respect individual rights. The decree divided liberals. Some believed this was the first step to serious reform; others recognised that it would never be implemented.

The Okhrana

Okhrana agents kept revolutionary parties under surveillance (see page 8). Additionally, Okhrana **agents provocateurs** infiltrated radical parties, stirring up divisions within the parties.

Illiteracy

Finally, the SRs and the RSDLP both relied on newspapers to spread their message. However, the vast majority of Russian peasants could not read, therefore it was difficult for radicals to influence groups such as the peasants.

Complete the paragraph

Look at this sample A-level exam question and a paragraph written in answer to this question. The paragraph contains a point and specific examples, but lacks a concluding analytical link back to the question. Complete the paragraph, adding this link in the space provided.

How far were divisions among the Tsar's opponents responsible for the survival of autocracy in Russia in the first decade of Nicholas II's rule?

> Divisions among the Tsar's opponents were partially responsible for the survival of autocracy in Russia between 1894 and 1904. First, these divisions meant that radicals could not work together. Liberals, who formed the League of Liberation in 1903, were committed to political change. However, SRs and Russia's Marxists in the RSDLP focused on social and economic revolution. As a result of these profound ideological differences it was impossible for liberals and socialists to work together. Secondly, the socialist movement was divided against itself. SRs and Marxists disagreed on the role of the peasants and workers in any revolution, and within each movement there were differences over tactics. The RSDLP was divided between Bolsheviks and Mensheviks, while the SRs were divided over the use of violence. Again, these divisions meant that parties on the left could not unite to oppose the Tsar. Overall,
>
> _____
>
> _____

Spectrum of importance

Look at the following sample AS and A-level exam questions and list of general points which could be used to answer the question. Use your own knowledge and the information on the opposite page to reach a judgement about the importance of these general points to the question posed. Write their numbers on the spectrum below to indicate their relative importance.

'The survival of Tsarism, in the years 1894–1904, was primarily due to the work of the Okhrana.' How far do you agree with this statement?

Was the Okhrana the main reason for the survival of Tsarism in the years 1894–1904? Explain your answer. **AS**

1 The work of the Okhrana

2 Russification

3 Anti-Semitism

4 The weaknesses of the opposition

Less important ⟵————————————————————⟶ Very important

Having done this, write a brief justification of your placement, explaining why some of these factors are more important than others. The resulting diagram could form the basis of an essay plan.

The 1905 Revolution

The Russo-Japanese War, which lasted from February 1904 until September 1905, was one of the main triggers of the 1905 Revolution.

The Russo-Japanese War

The war was caused by the Tsar's decision to try to expand the Russian Empire by invading China. This brought Russia into conflict with the Japanese Empire.

The Russo-Japanese War led to military defeat, economic problems, and exposed the weakness of Russia's leaders.

Military defeats

The racist Tsar assumed that Russia was bound to triumph over its Asian enemies. However:
- the Japanese inflicted humiliating defeats on the Russian army and navy
- the Russians were forced to surrender Port Arthur in January 1905
- the Russian Baltic fleet was defeated by the Japanese navy at the Battle of Tsushima in May 1905.

Economic and political problems

Russia's defeat was based on the fact that, while Japan had a highly advanced industrial economy and a well organised government, Russia had a backward economy and incompetent leaders.

Political consequences

The economic strain of fighting the war meant that the economy could no longer meet the needs of the Russian population. Food prices rose, while wages stayed the same. As a result workers began to organise strikes and protests.

The Russo-Japanese War exposed Nicholas II's incompetence. He:
- refused to listen to bad news from the war
- appointed deferential generals with little experience of modern warfare
- trusted his religious advisers who promised him that God would give Russia victory
- had little understanding of economics or modern military strategy
- rejected realistic assessments of the problems facing Russia from senior ministers such as Sergei Witte, who knew that the economy was too weak and the military leaders were too incompetent to cope with war.

Bloody Sunday

In January 1905 a priest called Father Gapon led 150,000 protestors to the **Winter Palace** to present a petition asking for better pay and conditions of work to the Tsar.

The march took place in the context of strikes and protests in St Petersburg caused by the war.

Massacre

In response to the march, local officials called in the army to maintain control. The soldiers opened fire on the crowd, leading to a massacre in which more than 200 people were killed and 800 wounded. The massacre became known as 'Bloody Sunday'.

The consequences of the massacre

The massacre helped to unite different groups. Bloody Sunday undermined the myth that the Tsar was a caring **'Little Father'** to the Russian people. Rather, radical propaganda argued that the massacre demonstrated that the Tsar cared nothing for the suffering of his people.

As a result of the massacre there were waves of protests. By February 1905, 400,000 workers were on strike in response to the massacre.

Father Gapon

Father Gapon played the leading role in organising the march to the Winter Palace. He also wrote the petition that the marchers intended to deliver to the Tsar. Gapon was a radical Orthodox priest who was sincerely concerned with improving the lives of the poor. Prior to the march Gapon organised the Assembly of Factory and Mill Workers of St Petersburg. The organisation quickly spread throughout the city. By 1905 it had 8,000 members. Initially, Gapon's organisation had been a 'Police Union', established as part of Zubatov's 'Police Socialism' initiative (see page 8). However, by 1905 the Okhrana had abandoned 'Police Socialism' and Gapon was working on his own initiative.

(i) Qualify your judgement

Below is a sample AS Level exam question with the accompanying source. Having read the question and the source, complete the following activity.

> How much weight do you give the evidence of Source 1 for an enquiry into the problems facing the Tsarist system during the Russo-Japanese War? Explain your answer using the source, the information given about it and your own knowledge of the historical context. **AS**

Below are three judgements about the value of Source 1 to a historian investigating the problems facing the Tsarist system during the Russo-Japanese War. Circle the judgement that best describes the value of the source, and explain why it is the best in the space provided.

1 Source 1 is valuable to a historian investigating the problems faced by the Tsarist regime because it reflects the opinion of a senior member of the government whose expertise in economics and foreign affairs mean that he was well placed to understand the difficulties the government faced.

2 Source 1 is unreliable to a historian because it is biased.

3 Source 1 is partially valuable to a historian investigating the problems faced by the Tsarist regime during the Russo-Japanese War, because it reflects the view of a senior member of the government, who was well placed to understand the deficiencies of the war effort. However, it is less useful for revealing popular discontent as it is focused on the working of the government.

The best judgement about the value of Source 1 is _____ because _____

_____

_____

SOURCE 1

From the memoirs of Sergei Witte, one of the Tsar's ministers and advisers. Witte served as Minister of Finance and a senior diplomat, therefore he understood Russia's economy and understood developments in the rest of the world.

In February 1905 our army, led by General Kuropatkin, suffered a striking defeat near Mukden. The battle was remarkable, both for the number of troops involved and for the severity of our defeat – the worst, as far as I can recall, in the history of our army. Because the debacle at Mukden revealed General Kuropatkin's complete inadequacy as commander-in-chief, he was replaced by the aged, poorly educated General Linevich. The chief reason for our failures against Japan was our lack of preparation for a war which we had provoked.

Our defeats, especially that at Mukden, roused all levels of the Russian population, in varying ways to be sure, against the government as the regime had shown itself to be weak and incompetent. The revolutionary mood at home, which became stronger with the news of each defeat, revealed itself in proclamations, meetings, and strikes, which spread from Russia to our troops in Asia.

My view that victory against Japan was no longer possible was supported by an article in *Russian Word*,* one of a series of intelligent articles on the course of the war. In it the anonymous author clearly demonstrated that it was impossible to expect any victories from Linevich. With his characteristic optimism the Tsar believed that new leadership could change the course of the war.

* *Russian Word*: a radical journal that published articles by liberals and socialists. It was banned in 1905.

The 1905 Revolution: the spread of revolutionary activity

Following Bloody Sunday, revolt spread across Russia. The 1905 Revolution was a series of spontaneous uprisings, not a co-ordinated attack on the Tsar's government.

Peasant revolt

In 1905 peasant resentment turned into revolution. By the summer of 1905 the authorities had lost control of around 15 per cent of rural Russia. Unrest started in the spring, and was worst in the 'Black Earth' region of western Russia.

Peasant unrest took many forms, including:
- violence against government officials, landowners and government property
- zemstvos' petitions demanding land, which were organised by moderate SRs
- land seizures.

National minorities

The Empire's national minorities, such as the Finns and the Poles, also rebelled. There were general strikes in the Baltic states and violence in cities such as Warsaw and Lodz in Poland.

The 1905 Revolution had a dramatic impact on Finland. By early November the Tsar had been forced to end the policy of Russification and restore Finland's traditional rights.

Military unrest

The mutiny of the *Battleship Potemkin* of June 1905 is the most famous example of revolutionary action in the Russian military. Sailors rebelled against their officers, and took control of the ship. The revolutionary sailors then sailed to Odessa where they fired on government forces which were trying to suppress the revolution in the city. The ship eventually fled to Romania.

At the end of the year there were mutinies of troops stationed in Russia's major cities, such as the mutiny of sailors at the **Kronstadt naval base** near St Petersburg in October.

Urban unrest

Strikes in Russia's cities broke out on a massive scale. Urban violence often focused on the Jews. The worst anti-Semitic violence took place in October in Odessa where at least 400 Jews were killed and over 1,600 Jewish homes were destroyed.

The St Petersburg Soviet

By autumn 1905 the revolution was becoming more radical. The Tsar's August Manifesto (see page 18) had failed to end the unrest. Indeed, a general strike developed between September and October of 1905. By the end of 1905 over 2.7 million workers were on strike.

The nature of the Soviet

In this context, workers established the St Petersburg Soviet, an elected committee comprising around 500 delegates, representing 200,000 workers across 147 factories. The majority of workers elected to the Soviet supported the Mensheviks.

The Soviet was initially set up in October 1905 to co-ordinate the strike. However, it soon took over important aspects of running the whole city.

The impact of the Soviet

The St Petersburg Soviet was the first of many. By the end of October, 50 towns across Russia, including Moscow and Odessa, had their own Soviets, linked to large-scale strikes.

The Soviet also started political campaigns. The Soviet campaigned for an eight-hour working day, and encouraged workers not to pay tax.

Trotsky's role

One of the reasons for the impact of the Soviet was the leadership of **Leon Trotsky**, an intellectual and revolutionary. Trotsky played a leading role among the members of the RSDLP who were part of the Soviet. He also helped the Soviet avoid confrontations with the government and employers by urging the Soviet to act pragmatically and abandon some of its more radical demands.

The end of the Soviet

The St Petersburg Soviet was closed by force in early December. Tsarist troops stormed a meeting of the Soviet while Trotsky was speaking.

In response a Bolshevik-led armed uprising took place in Moscow. The uprising was crushed by loyal Tsarist soldiers, leaving over a thousand dead.

By December 1905 the Tsar was in a stronger position. His October Manifesto (see page 18) won over the majority of middle-class liberals. Crushing the Soviet effectively brought the 1905 Revolution to an end. The Soviets in Moscow and Odessa were also suppressed by the Tsar's troops.

Select the detail

Below is a sample A-level exam question with the accompanying sources. Having read the question and the sources, complete the following activity.

How far could the historian make use of Sources 1 and 2 together to investigate the nature of the St Petersburg Soviet?

Below are three claims that you could make when answering the question. Read the claims and then select quotes from the sources to support them. Copy down the quotes in the space provided. Remember to keep the quotes short, never copy more than a sentence.

1 The St Petersburg Soviet represented Russian workers.

_____

_____

2 The St Petersburg Soviet made radical demands.

_____

_____

3 Ultimately the St Petersburg Soviet was not strong enough to achieve its aims.

_____

_____

SOURCE 1

From an essay by Trotsky on the 1905 Revolution, written in 1906.

On all the important questions – strikes, the struggle for the eight-hour working day, the arming of the workers – the initiative came not from the Soviet, but from the more advanced factories. Meetings of workers passed resolutions that were taken by deputies* to the Soviet. In this way, the organisation of the Soviet was an organisation of the overwhelming majority of St Petersburg's workers.

Representatives of the RSDLP did not have, either in the Soviet or the Executive Committee, a deciding vote. They participated in debates but not in voting. The Soviet was organised by the principle of representation of workers according to factory and profession – not according to Party groups. Party representatives could serve the Soviet by advising, based on their political experience and knowledge. However, they could not have a deciding vote, because that would break the principle of workers representing themselves.

* deputies: representatives

SOURCE 2

From Ariadna Tyrkova-Williams' book *Cheerful Giver*, published in 1935. The passage describes the dissolution of the St Petersburg Soviet in December 1905. Tyrkova-Williams was a Russian-born feminist writer and intellectual. She wrote for *Liberty*, the radical liberal newspaper founded in 1904 by Pyotr Struve. She was imprisoned for revolutionary activity in 1904, but returned to Russia in October 1905.

Complete disorder reigned. Excited, confused and amazed, the members of the first St Petersburg Soviet stood or shambled about against the chairs. The floor was covered with paper as the street was with snow.

When in the morning they read their Manifesto in the newspapers, they felt themselves daring revolutionaries, dictating their own will to the government. However, now confusion and defeat hung over them. At last we reached the door to find a gun pointing almost in our faces. We turned back. The crowd was thinning fast, as members of the Soviet were taken in batches to a holding room, where they were searched and escorted to prison.

Nicholas II's response

Nicholas II was unable to regain control of Russia until October 1905.

The failure of the August Manifesto

Nicholas began to show signs of compromise in August, with the publication of the August Manifesto, or 'Bulygin Constitution'. Nicholas' advisers, particularly Witte, hoped that the Manifesto would divide opposition and therefore become the first step towards ending the Revolution.

The August Manifesto promised to establish an elected consultative assembly, or Duma. It also set out a complex electoral system which gave all Russian men the right to vote, but ensured that the votes of the rich were worth more than the votes of the poor.

Liberal reaction

The August Manifesto failed to win over liberals. The vast majority of liberals rejected the Manifesto because:
● the proposed Duma was due to be **consultative** rather than **legislative**
● the electoral system excluded national minorities
● the electoral system did not include equal voting
● the Manifesto set no date for the first elections
● the Manifesto contained no guarantee of individual rights, or press freedom.

The proposal contained nothing to appease workers or peasants – indeed, Witte had no intention of compromising with Russia's poor. As a result, the August Manifesto did nothing to stop the protests of workers or peasants.

The October Manifesto

The Tsar was in an extremely weak position in October 1905. Opposition to his autocracy had grown since the summer. What is more the August Manifesto had alienated middle-class Russians.

The Tsar responded with the October Manifesto: a decree which introduced seemingly radical **constitutional reform**.

The Manifesto succeeded in winning over a significant section of the Russian middle class.

The October Manifesto promised major reforms:
● Greater freedom: the Manifesto promised that the government would respect individual rights, and allow greater press freedom, greater freedom of expression and **freedom of assembly**.
● Elected representation: the Manifesto promised almost universal suffrage for Russian men, with equal voting rights for rich and poor.
● An elected Duma with the power to approve or veto new laws.
● Political parties and trades unions would be legalised.

The response of opposition groups

The October Manifesto succeeded in dividing opposition to the Tsar.

The vast majority of liberals welcomed the October Manifesto as a major step towards a **constitutional monarchy**. Many hoped that the Manifesto would effectively end the Tsar's autocracy and establish a **liberal democratic regime**.

Radical liberals and socialists rejected the new Manifesto. For some liberals the reforms did not give enough power to the Duma. Socialists argued that the reforms failed to address the peasants' desire for land or the workers' need for better conditions. Indeed, the St Petersburg Soviet called a general strike to show their rejection of the compromise set out in the Manifesto.

Renewed violence

The Tsar was also aided by renewed violence. The Union of Russian People, founded in November 1905, and the **Black Hundreds** began pogroms against the Jews and street fights with striking workers. The Union of Russian People fought for 'Orthodoxy, Autocracy and Nationality', the key principles of Tsarism.

Racist violence increased during November and contemporary newspapers indicate that thousands of Jews were killed. This appeal to racist nationalism helped turn the tide of the Revolution, as patriotism was one of the main supports of Tsarism.

The Tsar's position in November

By mid-November opposition was split and the Tsar was in a much stronger position. However, the majority of Russia's workers were still on strike and Trotsky and the leaders of Russia's Soviets were determined to continue fighting for workers' rights.

Identify the concept

Below are five sample exam questions based on some of the following concepts:

- Cause – questions concern the reasons for something, or why something happened.
- Consequence – questions concern the impact of an event, an action or a policy.
- Change/continuity – questions ask you to investigate the extent to which things changed or stayed the same.
- Similarity/difference – questions ask you to investigate the extent to which two events, actions or policies were similar.
- Significance – questions concern the importance of an event, an action or a policy.

Read each of the sample Section B questions and work out which of the concepts they are based on:

1 'Opposition to Tsarism had little impact on Tsarist rule in the period prior to the 1905 Revolution.' How far do you agree with this statement?

2 How accurate is it to say that the 1905 Revolution was a turning point in Nicholas II's reign in the years 1894–1914

3 Were Russia's growing economic problems the main reason for the outbreak of the Revolution in January 1905? Explain your answer. **AS**

4 'Nicholas II's power was fundamentally weakened by the 1905 Revolution.' How far do you agree with this statement?

5 How accurate is it to say that Nicholas II's reactionary policies weakened the government of Russia in the years 1894–1905?

6 How significant was the work of the Okhrana for the stability of Tsarism in the years 1894–1904? **AS**

The flaw in the argument

Look at the following sample Section B exam question and a paragraph written in answer to this question. The paragraph contains an argument which attempts to answer the question. However, there is an error in the argument. Use your knowledge of this topic to identify the flaw in the argument.

'Opposition to Tsarism had little impact on Tsarist rule in the period prior to the 1905 Revolution.' How far do you agree with this statement?

> Liberal opposition had a major impact on Tsarist rule in the period prior to the 1905 Revolution. Russian liberals organised in the League of Liberation demanded major political reform. The League of Liberation's programme, published after its first congress in 1904, demanded an elected parliament with law-making powers and legal protection for individual rights. It also contained economic demands such as a maximum eight-hour working day for Russian workers. The League also campaigned for Russia's national minorities, demanding self-determination for groups such as the Finns and the Poles. Finally, Struve, one of the League's more radical members, argued for extensive social and economic rights for Russia's workers and peasants. In this way, liberal opposition had a major impact on Tsarist rule because it made radical political, social and economic demands.

The recovery of Tsarist power

By December the Tsar was in a much stronger position. However, the Tsar still faced opposition. Indeed, Lenin returned from exile in November 1905 and urged the St Petersburg Soviet to stage an armed uprising against the Tsar.

Returning troops

The end of the Russo-Japanese War allowed the Tsar's government to send the Russian army to crush workers' protests in the cities. Consequently, Nicholas ordered 100,000 troops to be recalled in order to end the Revolution.

The returning troops were loyal to the Tsar because they had not been exposed to radical propaganda. Additionally, the Ministry of War had given in to the demands of soldiers in order to win back their loyalty:

- Army pay was doubled.
- Soldiers' rations were increased.
- New clothing was issued.
- Soldiers were given bedding and handkerchiefs which were useful for first aid.

As a result mutinies in the army all but ceased in December.

Crushing the St Petersburg Soviet

In mid-December the government moved against the Soviet in a series of steps:

- First, the Okhrana arrested leading figures from the Soviet.
- Second, it declared **martial law**.
- Third, the police and army stormed factories and the meeting place of the Soviet, arresting rebel workers.

The end of the revolution?

Unrest continued into 1906; however, the suppression of the St Petersburg and Moscow Soviets destroyed the last hope of overthrowing the Tsar.

Why did the Tsar survive?

The Tsar survived for several reasons:

- For most of 1905 protests were unco-ordinated.
- The October Manifesto successfully divided opposition to the Tsar.
- Concessions to soldiers won the loyalty of the returning army.
- The workers of St Petersburg and Moscow were overwhelmed by the force of the returning troops.
- The Tsar had some popular support from the Union of Russian People and the Black Hundreds.

The extent of the recovery of Tsarist power

By December it was clear that the Tsar had the support of the army. This meant that he was able to crush rebellions by workers and peasants.

The electoral law

The extent of the Tsar's victory was clear from the Electoral Law of December 1905. The law failed to give the liberals what they wanted. Specifically:

- the Duma would be selected by **indirect elections**
- soldiers, women and some workers were not **enfranchised**
- votes were not equal: the electoral system gave more power to the rich.

Partial recovery?

However, autocracy was not fully restored. The reforms brought in at the end of 1905 placed limits on the Tsar's power:

- Political parties and trades unions were legalised. This allowed the formation of groups which could oppose the Tsar.
- The new Duma, introduced in 1906, could veto laws proposed by the Tsar. This ended his complete authority over law making in the Russian Empire.
- Peasant protest and protest in countries such as Poland and Finland continued into 1906. In this sense the Tsar had not re-established full control over the whole of his Empire.
- The Tsar had been forced to end his policy of Russification in Finland in order to end the protests of Finnish nationalists.

Was the 1905 Revolution a revolution?

The events of 1905 are regularly referred to as a 'revolution'. However, Marxists argue that the key feature of a revolution is that it transfers political and economic power from one class to another. Clearly, the 1905 Revolution failed to do this.

Other historians view a revolution as a fundamental and irreversible change. Evidently the events of 1905 created some change, but how far it transformed Russia is a matter of considerable debate.

ⓐ Identify key terms

Below is a sample Section B question which includes a key term or phrase. Key terms are important because their meaning can be helpful in structuring your answer, developing an argument, and establishing criteria that will help form the basis of a judgement.

> 'The essential features of autocracy survived the 1905 Revolution.' How far do you agree with this statement?

- First, identify the key word or term. This will be a word or phrase that is important to the meaning of the question. Underline the word or phrase.
- Second, define the key phrase. Your definition should set out the key features of the phrase or word that you are defining.
- Third, make an essay plan that reflects your definition.
- Finally, write a sentence answering the question that refers back to the definition.

Now repeat the task, and consider how the change in key terms affects the structure, argument and final judgement of your essay.

> 'The 1905 Revolution did not lead to radical reforms to the government of Nicholas II.' How far do you agree with this statement?

Support your judgement

Look at the following sample Section B question and two basic judgements. Read the exam question and the two judgements. Support the judgement that you agree with most strongly by adding a reason that justifies the judgement.

> 'The essential features of autocracy survived the 1905 Revolution.' How far do you agree with this statement?

Overall, the essential features of autocracy survived the 1905 Revolution in the sense that . . .

_____

_____

The reforms to the Tsar's government introduced at the end of 1905 did not alter the essential features of autocracy because . . .

_____

_____

Tips:

- You should consider which features of the Tsar's government were *essential to autocracy* and which were not.
- Whichever option you choose you will have to weigh up both sides of the argument. You could use words such as 'whereas' and 'although' in order to help the process of evaluation.

Exam focus (AS Level)

Below is an AS Level Section A exam-style question and answer. Read the response and the comments around it.

Why is Source 1 valuable to the historian for an enquiry into the grievances of the people of St Petersburg in early 1905?

Explain your answer using the source, the information given about it and your own knowledge of the historical context.

SOURCE 1

Petition Prepared for Presentation to Nicholas II. The petition was drawn up by Father Georgii Gapon, who planned to present it to the Tsar as part of the march that he planned for 9 January 1905. After the Tsar's soldiers opened fire on the unarmed marchers the day became known as Bloody Sunday.

Sovereign!

We, workers and inhabitants of the city of St Petersburg, our wives, children, and helpless old parents, have come to you, Sovereign, to seek justice and protection. We are impoverished and oppressed, we are burdened with work, and insulted. We are treated not like humans [but] like slaves who must suffer a bitter fate and keep silent. And we have suffered, but we only get pushed deeper and deeper into a gulf of misery, ignorance, and lack of rights. Despotism and arbitrariness are suffocating us, we are gasping for breath. Sovereign, we have no strength left. We have reached the limit of our patience. We have come to that terrible moment when it is better to die than to continue unbearable sufferings.

The source is valuable for an enquiry into the grievances of the St Petersburg people as it was written primarily by Gapon, who understood the problems of the poor. Second, over 3,000 people, possibly as many as 50,000, marched to deliver the petition to the Tsar, indicating that it reflected a large section of the population. Finally, the Petition was part of wider protest which also indicates the situation was dire for working people.

The Petition was written by Gapon, who was deeply involved with efforts to improve the lives of the poor. Gapon organised the Assembly of Factory and Mill Workers of St Petersburg, an organisation with branches across the city and 8,000 members. In this way, the Petition is useful for understanding the grievances of the people in St Petersburg because its author had considerable experience of the conditions of working people in the capital, and their desire for change.

The Petition is also useful for understanding grievances as it reflected a cross-section of St Petersburg. The Petition was written to the Tsar from the 'workers ... our wives, children, and helpless old parents'. Indeed, it was a deliberate strategy to include women, children and the elderly in the march to show the unity of people of the capital. It is reasonable to infer that the support for the march, which came from a wide cross-section of the capital's population, indicates that the grievances set out in the Petition reflected the feelings of the people of St Petersburg at the time.

This is a focused introduction that outlines the structure of the rest of the essay.

The essay uses detailed knowledge of the historical context to make inferences about the usefulness of the source.

Here the answer selects aspects of the source which supports the point being made. It also explains the meaning and significance of the quote in its historical context.

Here the answer explains and makes a reasoned inference from a key phrase in the source, which is related directly to the question.

Finally, the Petition was written at a time of unrest in the capital. The Russo-Japanese War created economic hardship. This may, in part, explain why the Petition claims that Russian workers were 'impoverished'. Additionally, there were major strikes in St Petersburg. By early January 1905, 150,000 workers were on strike and the capital had no electricity or newspapers. The scale of the strikes indicates that the workers of St Petersburg had genuine grievances and indicates that the dramatic language, which claims that workers were treated like 'slaves', and were 'pushed deeper and deeper into a gulf of misery' truly reflects the grievances of many people in the capital.

In conclusion there is much of value in the source for an enquiry into the grievances of the people of St Petersburg in early 1905 because its author understood the feelings of the capital's population, it was supported by a cross-section of St Petersburg and it was written at a time when grievances had caused a general strike.

Here knowledge of historical context is used to show one way in which the source is useful.

The conclusion summarises the ways in which the source is useful, and the key reasons for its usefulness.

This response has a strong focus upon the question and gives three clear reasons why the source is useful for the enquiry. Passages from the source, a consideration of the source's context and the nature, origin and purpose of the source are used to make valid inferences.

Consolidation (sources)

It is useful to analyse sample answers such as this by colour coding:
- Contextual knowledge
- Inferences
- Quotes and Paraphrases from Source 1
- Analysis of Utility.

This helps to recognise the relationship between each component part of the answer, and gives ideas on how such answers can be constructed.

Exam focus (A-level)

Below is a sample exam question answer to an A-level Section A question. Read the model response and the comments around it.

Study Sources 1 and 2. How far could the historian make use of Sources 1 and 2 together to investigate the attitude of the Russian government to the St Petersburg Soviet in late 1905? Explain your answer, using both sources, the information given about them and your own knowledge of the historical context.

SOURCE 1

From *The Memoirs of Count Witte* published in New York in 1921. Sergei Witte was one of the Tsar's most trusted advisers, and the author of the October Manifesto.

The City of St Petersburg, the intellectual capital of the country, with its large industrial population was, naturally enough, one of the chief storm centres of the revolution. It was there that the Soviet of Workingmen's Deputies came into being. The idea of setting up this institution was born in the early days of October and the press began to campaign for it among the working population of the capital. The first session of the Soviet took place at the Technological Institute. At this session an appeal was issued to the workmen of the capital, urging them to form extreme political demands. At this session a Jew was elected as president of the Soviet.

The historic manifesto which granted the country a constitution was issued in October 1905. At the time the Soviet appeared to be a considerable power for the reason that it was obeyed by the working masses.

The Soviet decided to declare a general strike, as an expression of the workers' dissatisfaction with the October Manifesto.

In November, I ordered the arrest of the whole Soviet. As soon as the Soviet gathered all 190 members were rounded up and arrested. Thus ended the affair of the Soviet.

SOURCE 2

From an account of the Moscow uprising by A.V. Sokolov, a Bolshevik activist. Here Sokolov describes preparations to defend the Moscow Soviet from the Tsar's troops, following news that the St Petersburg Soviet had been crushed.

Bolshevik, Menshevik and Socialist Revolutionary organisers argued until they were hoarse over what methods should be used during the revolution – 'mass agitation' or 'vanguard action'. While this was going on the crowd of workers assembled in the factory hall sat and waited for directions from their leaders. They waited for an hour then two while the leaders argued, the subject of the argument becoming ever more obscure. Eventually the workers began to leave for the streets.

A crowd approached the police chief's house and began shooting at the windows. After several warnings, troops responded with artillery fire. The army killed several people and injured others. The shooting continued for three hours. The distraught crowd continued to fire back at the troops. Shots injured quite a few onlookers. Army patrols completely surrounded the workers, blocking their escape.

Both Sources 1 and 2 are fairly useful to a historian investigating the attitude of the Russian government to the St Petersburg Soviet in late 1905. Source 1 comes from Sergei Witte, the head of the Russian government at the time. In this sense, it gives the view of the most senior of the Tsar's ministers. Moreover, it gives Witte's attitude to the origins, demands and suppression of the Soviet. Source 2 comes from a very different perspective, that of a Bolshevik activist. However, it is useful in that it shows that the government were prepared to use lethal force against the Soviet.

Source 1 demonstrates a number of Witte's attitudes to the Soviet. First, it shows that he believed the Soviet came about due to the influence of intellectuals and working people. He writes that as a result of the intellectual and urban character of the city it was 'naturally enough, one of the chief storm centres of the revolution'. Witte's assertion about the nature

The essay opens with a clear focus on the question.

The introduction sets out a range of ways in which the sources are useful, and summarises the key difference in their perspectives.

of the Soviet is backed up by Source 2 which notes that the Soviet was full of 'Bolshevik, Menshevik ... organisers'. These parties were popular among the working class, and they debated 'mass agitation' or 'vanguard action', which indicates they were aware of intellectual debates going on in the Russian Social Democratic and Labour Party. In this sense, the sources together are useful because they indicate that Witte's attitude about the reasons for the emergence of the Soviet were broadly accurate.

Source 1 is also useful for showing Witte's attitude towards the demands of the Soviet. He writes that the Soviet put forward 'extreme political demands'. From Witte's point of view the demand for an eight-hour day and a refusal to pay tax must have seemed extreme. His own October Manifesto was a much less radical document, as it promised no economic changes at all. This is not how the leaders of the Soviet saw their demands. Leon Trotsky, an intellectual and revolutionary and leader of the Soviet, tried to minimise confrontation with the government and urged the Soviet to adopt what he considered to be moderate demands. Nonetheless, Source 1 shows that Trotsky's policy failed, as Witte viewed the Soviet as 'extreme'.

However, Source 1 is less useful for showing how the government responded to the Soviet. It only says that 'I ordered the arrest of the whole Soviet ... all 190 members were rounded up and arrested.' In reality the government's actions were much more ruthless and extreme. Here Source 2 is more useful as it describes the extreme violence used by government forces during the repression of the Soviet. According to Source 2, 'troops responded with artillery fire. The army killed several people and injured others. The shooting continued for three hours.' The use of artillery shows that the government were prepared to be extremely brutal. Source 1 makes no acknowledgement of this. Rather Source 1 portrays the government as moderate and constructive as it issued the 'historic manifesto which granted the country a constitution', a reference to the October Manifesto, whereas it portrays the Soviet as 'extreme'. In this sense, Source 1 is misleading as it implies that the government was moderate. Source 2's claim that the government used brutal methods is plausible as from the context we know that the Tsarist regime often used barbaric methods to deal with political threats. Moreover, Tsarist forces used artillery against the Moscow Soviet. Once again this contextual knowledge makes the claim of Source 2 plausible.

In conclusion, Source 1 and 2 are both quite useful for investigating the attitude of the Russian government to the St Petersburg Soviet in late 1905. They show that the government had a good idea about the origins of the Soviet, and they indicate that from the point of view of the head of government the Soviet demands were extreme. Nonetheless, Source 1's account of the suppression of the Soviet is much less reliable – it implies that Witte's attitude was moderate and humane, whereas Source 2 shows clearly that the government was prepared to use overwhelming violence to crush the Soviet.

Side annotations:

The sources are used together to evaluate the usefulness of Source 1's claim about the origins of the Soviet.

This passage evaluates Witte's claim about the Soviet's 'extreme' demands in the historical context of Witte's values and assumptions.

This passage evaluates the reliability of both sources using historical context to make a reasoned judgement.

The conclusion summarises the argument of the essay and reaches a supported overall judgement.

This is a strong answer as it interrogates the evidence of both sources, making intelligent inferences. It uses historical context to weigh the evidence of both sources and in so doing comes to a supported judgement about the value of different aspects of the sources.

Consolidation (sources)

It is useful to analyse sample answers such as this by colour coding:
- Contextual knowledge
- Inferences
- Quotes and Paraphrases from Source 1
- Quotes and Paraphrases from Source 2
- Analysis of Utility.

This helps to recognise the relationship between each component part of the answer, and gives ideas on how such answers can be constructed.

2 The end of Romanov rule, 1906–17

Change and continuity in government

The 1905 Revolution did not lead to the radical changes that many had hoped. Nonetheless, Tsarism was forced to embrace some limited reform.

The Fundamental Laws

In April 1906 the Tsar attempted to reassert his authority. He **promulgated** the Fundamental Laws – in essence, a new constitution. The Tsar was in a stronger position in April than he had been in October 1905, as his opponents were divided and the workers had been crushed. Consequently, the Fundamental Laws re-emphasised the autocratic nature of Russian government.

The Tsar's powers

The Fundamental Laws gave the Tsar extensive powers:
- Article 4 stated that the Tsar had absolute, God-given autocratic power.
- The Tsar retained sole authority over command of the army and dealings with foreign nations.
- Article 87 set out the nature of the Tsar's relationship with the new Duma. The Tsar retained 'supreme sovereign power'. This meant that Nicholas had the right to make laws without consultation with the Duma. Nonetheless, the Duma was given the right to **ratify** the Tsar's laws.
- The Tsar was given the right to dissolve the Duma and call new elections at any time.

The Duma

The 1906 constitution altered the nature of Russian government:
- It created a **bicameral** Duma.
- The lower house of the Duma was elected by an electorate made up of most male Russians.
- The upper house, known as the 'Council of State', was partially appointed by the Tsar. The other half of the council was appointed by institutions such as the Orthodox Church.
- The upper house had the right to veto laws proposed by the lower house.
- It guaranteed individuals rights to freedom of expression, freedom of assembly, **freedom of conscience**, the right to form political parties and unions, as well as freedom of the press.

Reactions to the Fundamental Laws

The new constitution failed to satisfy liberals:
- The limited powers of the Duma did not fulfil the demands of liberals as the elected lower house did not have ultimate law-making power.
- Liberals recognised that the promise of individual rights was largely meaningless.

Socialists also argued that the new constitution failed to address Russia's underlying problems. The SRs argued that the new constitution did nothing to satisfy the peasants' desire for land, and Lenin argued that they would not limit the oppression of the working class.

The radicalism of the First Duma

The First Duma was elected in April 1906. It was largely made up of conservative **Octoberists**, the liberal **Kadets** and the **Troudoviks**. The SRs and the factions of the RSDLP boycotted the election.

The newly elected Duma made a series of radical demands:
- The creation of universal suffrage.
- Land reform.
- Freedom for **political prisoners**.

The Tsar dissolved this parliament after 73 days because they were making too many radical demands.

The Vyborg Manifesto

Led by the Kadets, radicals from the First Duma fled to the Finnish town of Vyborg. Kadets assumed that they would be safe from persecution while in Finland as the Tsar had promised to respect the traditional rights of the Finns.

Kadet radicals issued an **open letter**, 'the Vyborg Manifesto', which called on the Russian people to refuse to pay tax until the Duma was re-established.

However, Russian workers and peasants did not support the middle-class Kadets, as the middle class had compromised with the Tsar in late 1905. The Manifesto failed to have an impact and the Kadets who had organised the protest were imprisoned.

The failure of the First Duma and the Vyborg Manifesto led many Russian people to lose faith in liberal reform. Consequently, the Kadets lost popular support and public opinion became polarised between revolutionaries on the left and reactionaries on the right.

Quick quizzes at **www.hoddereducation.co.uk/myrevisionnotes**

Select the detail

Below is a sample A-level exam question with the accompanying sources. Having read the question and the sources, complete the following activity.

How far could the historian make use of Sources 1 and 2 together to investigate the extent of reform to the Tsarist system introduced in 1906?

Below are three claims that you could make when answering the question. Read the claims and then select quotes from the sources to support them. Copy down the quotes in the space provided. Remember to keep the quotes short, never copy more than a sentence.

1 The reforms did not fundamentally limit the Tsar's autocratic power.

2 Individual rights were not truly guaranteed by the new constitution.

3 The 1906 reforms failed to live up to the promises given in 1905.

SOURCE 1

From the October Manifesto, published by Tsar Nicholas II in October 1905.

We, Nicholas II, Emperor and Autocrat of All the Russians, Tsar of Poland, Grand Duke of Finland, declare to all our loyal subjects. We have ordered the government to take the following steps in fulfilment of our unbending will:

Fundamental civil freedoms will be granted to the population, including real personal inviolability, freedom of conscience, speech, assembly and association.

Without halting the elections that have already been scheduled, participation in the Duma will be granted to those classes of the population which are at present deprived of voting powers (insofar as is possible in the short period before its convocation).

Further development of a universal franchise will be left to the newly established legislature (i.e. according to the law of August 6, 1905, to the Duma and Council of State).

It is established as an unshakeable rule that no law can come into force without its approval by the State Duma and representatives of the people will be given the opportunity to take real part in the supervision of the legality of authorities appointed by Us.

SOURCE 2

From the Fundamental Laws promulgated in April 1906.

Chapter I. The Essence of the Supreme Autocratic Power

The All-Russian Emperor possesses the supreme autocratic power. Not only fear and conscience, but God himself, commands obedience to his authority.

The sovereign emperor exercises power in conjunction with the State Council and the State Duma.

The sovereign emperor possesses the initiative in all legislative matters.

The sovereign emperor approves laws; and without his approval no legislative measure can become law.

The sovereign emperor takes charge of all the external relations of the Russian State. He determines the direction of Russia's foreign policy.

The sovereign emperor is the Commander-in-Chief of the Russian army and navy.

Chapter II. Rights and Obligations of Russian Subjects

Within the limits determined by law everyone can express his thoughts orally or in writing, as well as distribute these thoughts through publication or other means.

Exceptions to the rights outlined in this chapter include localities where martial law is declared or where there exist exceptional conditions that are determined by special laws.

Chapter IV. The Duma

The State Duma consists of members elected by the population of the Russian Empire for a period of five years.

No new law can come into force without the approval of the State Council and State Duma and the ratification of the sovereign emperor.

Nicholas II's relations with the Dumas, 1906–14

The Second Duma

A Second Duma was elected in 1907. The make-up of the Second Duma was quite different to the first:

- The Bolsheviks, Mensheviks and SRs took part in the election, therefore the Second Duma had a more radical make-up than the First.
- The Kadets lost a considerable proportion of their support.
- Right-wing parties who supported the autocracy also gained support.

As a result, the Second Duma was split between conservatives and radicals. The Octoberists worked with **Stolypin** to pass important land reform laws (see page 32). However, SRs, Bolsheviks and Mensheviks rejected Stolypin's proposed reforms. The police claimed that Bolshevik members of the Duma were encouraging mutinies. The Tsar used this as a pretext to dismiss the Duma after three months.

The Tsar and the Dumas, 1907

The first two Dumas had exposed the limits of the 1905–06 reforms, as well as the popular desire for greater economic and political reform. Consequently, they undermined the authority of the Tsar by exposing the true nature of his government.

Stolypin's solution to this problem was to introduce a new electoral law which guaranteed a conservative majority in the Duma.

Stolypyn's electoral law

Stolypyn's electoral law created a weighted voting system. The vast majority of Russian men could still vote, but the new system over-represented the aristocracy and middle class, while it under-represented the working class.

The Third and Fourth Dumas

The election of 1907 produced a conservative-dominated Duma as Stolypin had hoped. The Third Duma (1907–12) did not demand major reforms and broadly supported Stolypin's policies. Consequently, the Third Duma became known as the 'Stolypin Duma' or the 'Duma of Lords and Lackeys'. The Third Duma lasted for the full five years specified in the Russian constitution. It was replaced by the Fourth Duma (1912–17). The Fourth Duma was essentially as conservative as the Third.

Nicholas and the Duma

In spite of their conservative nature, Nicholas was unwilling to work with the later Dumas. Nicholas recognised that the Duma presented fundamental problems for autocratic rule:

- Autocracy was based on the view that the Tsar was the perfect representative of the Russian people. However, the Duma also claimed to represent the people of Russia. This undermined the Tsar's authority.
- The Duma gave Nicholas' opponents a public position of authority from which they could attack the Tsar's government. For example, Alexander Guchkov, leader of the Octoberists, attacked the Tsar's dependence on **Grigori Rasputin**.
- The Duma conducted research and wrote reports on aspects of the Tsar's rule. This meant that the Tsar's authority was challenged by experts.

The impact of the Dumas

The Third and Fourth Dumas were able to initiate a number of changes which improved Russian government.

- Land Captains were replaced by more **Justices of the Peace**. As a result the zemstvos were able to reassert their authority over local administration.
- A plan to establish universal primary education was introduced.
- Some health and accident insurance programmes were developed to help workers.
- Some improvements to the Russian armed forces were implemented.

The successes of the Dumas were a problem for the Tsar, as they suggested that the Dumas should play a larger role in Russian government. In this sense the Duma's victories undermined the Tsar's authority.

Complete the paragraph

Look at the following sample A-level exam question and a paragraph written in answer to this question. The paragraph contains a point and specific examples, but lacks a concluding analytical link back to the question. Complete the paragraph, adding this link in the space provided.

How significant were the Fundamental Laws in the survival of the Tsar's autocracy in the years 1906–14?

While the Fundamental Laws played an important role in reasserting the Tsar's autocracy, they also created new problems. The first two Dumas clashed with the government, exposing the limits of the Tsar's commitment to political reform and individual rights. For example, the First Duma was dissolved after it clashed with the government over issues such as land reform, democratisation and the freeing of political prisoners. Equally, a large number of the representatives who were elected to the Second Duma were SRs, Bolsheviks and Mensheviks who tried to block Stolypin's reforms. Therefore ...

_____

_____

Identify the concept a

Below are five sample exam questions based on some of the following concepts:
- Cause – questions concern the reasons for something, or why something happened.
- Consequence – questions concern the impact of an event, an action or a policy.
- Change/continuity – questions ask you to investigate the extent to which things changed or stayed the same.
- Similarity/difference – questions ask you to investigate the extent to which two events, actions or policies were similar.
- Significance – questions concern the importance of an event, an action or a policy.

Read each of the questions and work out which of the concepts they are based on.

1 How significant were the Fundamental Laws in the survival of the Tsar's autocracy in the years 1906–14?

2 How far was the 1905 Revolution a turning point in Tsarist government, in the period 1894–1914?

3 How far did the Fundamental Laws of 1906 reassert the essential features of Tsarist autocracy?

4 To what extent did the Fundamental Laws achieve Nicholas II's aims in the period 1906–14? AS

5 Was the 1905 Revolution the main reason for the introduction of the Fundamental Laws in April 1906? AS

Stolypin's repression, 1906–14

Between 1906 and 1911 Stolypin acted as the Tsar's head of government. Stolypin attempted to restore order through a policy of cautious reform and brutal repression.

Stolypin's repression

In August 1906 Stolypin declared a **state of emergency**. This formally suspended the rights guaranteed by the Fundamental Laws, allowing the government to use terror against the Tsar's subjects:

- Officials were given the right to imprison people without putting them on trial.
- The military were given the power to dispense justice. Lawyers and appeals were banned in military courts. Military courts had the right to exile or execute rebels, and appeals were not permitted.

The scale of repression

Between 1906 and 1910 Stolypin's courts found 37,620 people guilty of political crimes. Of these 8,640 were sent to labour camps and 1,858 were resettled to Russia's deserts or to the frozen wastes of Siberia. In the majority of these cases 'resettlement' meant death. Russia's prison population rose from 98,000 in 1905 to over 250,000 by 1913.

Stolypin's name became associated with the brutal policies. The trains that carried people away into exile became known as 'Stolypin wagons', and the hangman's noose was nicknamed 'Stolypin's necktie'.

Actions against revolutionary parties

Action against revolutionary parties came in two main phases.

1906–07

From 1906–07 repression of revolutionaries was widespread and brutal. The state's main method was to put revolutionaries on trial in military courts (see **Stolypin's repression** above).

Revolutionaries responded in two ways:

- The SRs continued their campaign of assassinations, leading to the deaths of 1,126 government officials in 1906.
- Revolutionary leaders fled Russia. Lenin, for example, fled to Finland and then to Western Europe.

1907–14

At the beginning of 1907 Maksimilian Trusevich, head of the Russian police, established eight regional security bureaus to target revolutionary parties. The new bureaus oversaw the dissolution of the Second Duma and the arrest and prosecution of the revolutionaries who had been elected to the Duma.

However, from mid-1907 Trusevich instituted a policy of surveillance and subversion. He tried to limit the number of executions, and disrupt revolutionary parties through infiltration.

This policy was highly effective and official reports indicate that Trusevich and Stolypin were convinced that, by 1908, their agents had effectively won the battle against revolutionary parties. Trusevich's agents infiltrated revolutionary parties, creating an atmosphere of mistrust, as revolutionaries had no idea which of their comrades were double agents. Evno Azef was one example of this kind of infiltration. In 1909 the SRs discovered that Azef, one of their most high-profile leaders, was a police informant. By 1913 Trusevich had 94 agents within revolutionary groups in St Petersburg alone.

Middle-class reaction

The Octoberists and right-wing parties supported the repressions. Even some liberals co-operated with the regime, as they did not want Russia to slide into anarchy.

Police failings

While the police were broadly effective at disrupting revolutionary parties, they failed to stamp out revolutionary newspapers. The Fundamental Laws effectively created a free press in Russia. In 1912 the Bolsheviks founded *Pravda* and the Mensheviks founded *Luch*. The police kept the newspapers under surveillance, and they attempted to close *Pravda* eight times between 1912 and 1914. However, *Pravda* always re-emerged.

Write the question

The following sources relate to Stolypin's policies as head of the Russian government. Having read the previous pages about Stolypin, write an exam-style question using the sources.

1 How far could the historian make use of Sources 1 and 2 together to investigate ...?

_____

_____

Explain your answer, using both sources, the information given about them and your own knowledge of the historical context.

2 Why is Source 1 valuable to the historian for an enquiry into ...?

_____

Explain your answer using the source, the information given about it and your own knowledge of the historical context. **AS**

SOURCE 1

From the memoirs of Alexander Izvolsky, Russian Foreign Minister from 1906 to 1910. Izvolsky was friends with, and a supporter of Stolypin. He was critical of the Kadets for being too radical, but like Stolypin, Izvolsky believed that limited reform was essential in order to stabilise and modernise Russia.

The Emperor's decision, not only to dissolve the [First] Duma, but at the same time to put Mr Stolypin at the head of the Government was a sudden, unexpected move that no one had foreseen.

The situation was unnecessarily complicated by the thoughtless attitude adopted by a great number of the deputies of the Duma, for which I hold the Kadet Party responsible. One hundred and ninety members of the Duma met in Finland, and there signed the Vyborg Manifesto.

Stolypin has the good judgement not to take the Vyborg prank seriously. He let the signers of the Manifesto return to St Petersburg unmolested, and only as a matter of principle, instituted legal proceedings against them, which resulted in making the principal leaders of the Kadets ineligible for election to the next Duma.

During 1906 and 1907 Stolypin came out of his first crisis with honour. Revolts were suppressed without excessive severity. Moreover, by conferring upon the Russian peasants the right of individual ownership of land, Stolypin created a new status for the peasants. In short, the peasants were no longer a class apart, they became for the first time Russian citizens.

SOURCE 2

From Lenin's article _'Stolypin and the Revolution'_. The article was written in response to Stolypin's assassination, and was published in October 1911 in a German revolutionary newspaper.

The assassination of the arch-hangman Stolypin occurred at a time when the Russian counter-revolution was coming to an end.

Stolypin was the head of the counter-revolutionary government for about five years, from 1906 to 1911. This was indeed a unique period crowded with instructive events. Stolypin the pogrom-monger groomed himself for a ministerial post in the only way in which a tsarist governor could; by torturing the peasants, by organising pogroms and by showing an ability to conceal these 'practices' behind glib phrases, poses and gestures.

The Stolypin period of the Russian counter-revolution is characterised specifically by the fact that the liberal bourgeoisie had been turning its back on democracy, and that Stolypin _was able to turn_ for assistance, sympathy, and advice first to one then to another representative of this bourgeoisie. Stolypin not only represented the dictatorship of the feudal landlords, Stolypin was minister during a period when counter-revolutionary sentiments prevailed among the _entire_ liberal bourgeoisie, including the Kadets.

Stolypin helped the Russian people to learn a useful lesson: either march to freedom by overthrowing the tsarist monarchy, under the leadership of the proletariat; or sink deeper into slavery, under the ideological and political leadership of the Kadets and Octoberists.

Stolypin's reforms, 1906–14

Stolypin's policies were not wholly repressive. Indeed, he did introduce key economic reforms. Stolypin understood that making more peasants small landowners would strengthen the government in two ways:

1 They would prevent the peasants supporting revolutionary groups in order to protect their property.
2 Limited land reform would help make Russian agriculture more productive, and in so doing increase the nation's wealth.

Land reform

Stolypin's land reform was designed to create a class of conservative landowning peasants. Stolypin hoped that as peasants began to own land, they would want to protect their property and make a profit, therefore they would abandon revolutionary radicalism and support the government.

1906 reforms

In 1906 Stolypin introduced important economic reforms. The new reforms:
- made it easier for peasants to break away from communes and establish independent farms
- encouraged the Peasant Land Bank to give more loans to peasants, in order to buy land and modern farming equipment.

Stolypin also provided incentives and government loans for peasants to move to land that had not been farmed in areas such as in Siberia.

Emigration to Siberia

Conditions in much of Siberia were extremely difficult. However, Siberia was rich in minerals and in the south-west there was a large amount of potential farmland. Consequently, Stolypin introduced incentives to encourage peasants to migrate to Siberia and farm the land. These included:
- cheap land
- interest-free loans
- cheap rail travel to Siberia.

Stolypin also initiated a publicity campaign to encourage peasants to set up home in Siberia.

Impact of Stolypin's reforms

Stolypin's reforms had a significant impact on the Russian economy. However, they were not wholly successful:

Successes	Failures
• In 1905, 20% of peasants owned land. By 1915 this had increased to 50%. • Agricultural production increased from 45.9 million tonnes in 1906 to 61.7 million tonnes in 1913. • Between 1906 and 1914, 25% of peasants had left the *mirs* (communes). • Between 1906 and 1913, 3.5 million peasants set up home in Siberia. • 80% of migrants to Siberia settled. • The use of fertilisers, machines, tools and crop rotation increased crop production across the Empire.	• The majority of peasants who accepted Stolypin's incentives were located in the more prosperous areas of Russia, such as southern Russia and the Ukraine. • His land reforms had a limited impact in the cities.

⊕ Identify key terms   a

Below is a sample Section B question which includes a key word or term. Key terms are important because their meaning can be helpful in structuring your answer, developing an argument, and establishing criteria that will help form the basis of a judgement.

'Between 1906 and 1914 the Tsar's government was wholly reactionary.' How far do you agree with this statement?

- First, identify the key word or term. This will be a word or phrase that is important to the meaning of the question. Underline the word or phrase.
- Second, define the key phrase. Your definition should set out the key features of the phrase or word that you are defining.
- Third, make an essay plan that reflects your definition.
- Finally, write a sentence answering the question that refers back to the definition.

Now repeat the task, and consider how the change in key terms affects the structure, argument and final judgement of your essay.

How accurate is it to say that by 1914 the Tsar's government was stable and strong?

⊕ Support your judgement

Look at the following sample exam question and two basic judgements. Read the exam question and the two judgements. Support the judgement that you agree with most strongly by adding a reason that justifies the judgement.

How accurate is it to say that by 1914 the Tsar's government was stable and strong?

1 Overall, the Tsar's government was largely stable by 1914 because …

_____

_____

2 The Tsar's government was broadly strong by 1914 because …

_____

_____

Tip: whichever option you choose you will have to weigh up both sides of the argument. You could use words such as 'whereas' and 'although' in order to help the process of evaluation.

The last years of peace

The Lena Goldfields strike and the ensuing massacre was one of a number of major industrial conflicts that took place in the Tsar's last years.

Unionisation

From 1906 to 1914 Russia's workers were increasingly unionised. Strikes occurred sporadically from 1906 to 1911, and increased significantly in the last years of peace, with major waves of strikes in 1912 and early 1914.

The Lena Goldfields

The Lena Goldfields mines were located in Siberia and controlled by the Lenzoloto Mining Company.

Causes of the strike

Workers had a series of long-term grievances which contributed to the strike. While the Lenzoloto Mining Company provided their workers with some benefits, housing and food were often of extremely low quality. In addition, the working day was either eleven or eleven and a half hours, depending on the season. Serving rotten horsemeat in the canteen was the trigger for the strike.

Striking workers quickly drew up a list of demands including:

- an eight-hour day
- sick pay
- a 30 per cent wage increase
- paid overtime
- better quality food
- respect from company officials.

The owners of the Lenzoloto Company refused to meet the workers' demands.

Massacre

The leaders of the miners were politically moderate, refused to use violence and repeatedly stated that they were willing to reach a compromise. However, the mine's management asked the police and the army to break up the strike.

Initially, the police arrested the strike's leaders. The miners responded with a protest march. The army reacted by opening fire on the unarmed miners, leading to 172 deaths and a similar number of injuries.

Aftermath

The massacre caused outrage. The Russian press condemned the massacre, as did politicians including Octoberists and Kadets.

The strike did not lead to a significant improvement of conditions in the Lena Goldfields. Unable to recruit enough Russian labour, the Lenzoloto Company employed workers from China and Korea.

Union militancy

The Lena Goldfield massacre of April 1912 was a turning point in the Russian union movement. From 1912 to 1914 the union movement was more assertive and strikes increased:

	Workers on strike
1912	750,000
1913	887,000
1914 January to July	1,450,000

Female tobacco and textile workers were some of the most radical workers during this period.

The nature of Tsarist government in 1914

By 1914 the exact nature of Tsarist government was controversial. Octoberists such as Guchkov claimed that the Tsar was part of a **constitutional government**. Socialists disagreed, arguing that Russia remained an autocracy.

Autocracy restored

There is evidence that autocracy was largely restored after 1905:
- The powers of the new Duma were minimal.
- Stolypin's state of emergency allowed the Tsar to ignore individual rights.

Growing democracy?

However, there are also some indications that Russian government was democratising. First, the later Dumas were able to scrutinise the Tsar's government. Scrutiny took the following forms:
- Members of the Duma had the right to question ministers and expose problems with the Tsar's government.
- Duma committees monitored key areas of government policy. For example, the Third Duma set up a military committee in 1907. The committee, chaired by Guchkov, examined military spending, leading to changes in policy in 1911.

Second, by 1914 Russia had a largely free press, which published criticisms of the Tsar.

Finally, the emergence of independent trades unions and political parties led to the development of civil society (see page 6).

Partial autocracy?

Clearly, Russia remained largely autocratic. Nonetheless, the Duma's power of scrutiny and the emergence of the free press meant that the Tsar no longer had total freedom of action.

Add the context

Below is a sample A-level exam question with the accompanying sources. Having read the question and the sources, complete the following activity.

> How far could the historian make use of Sources 1 and 2 together to investigate the conditions of workers at the Lena Goldfields in 1911–12?

First, look for aspects of the source that refer to the events and discussion that were going on around the time that the source was written. Underline the key phrases and write a brief description of the context in the margin next to the source. Draw an arrow from the key phrase to the context. Try to find three key phrases in each source.

Tip: look at the information above the source – you should contextualise this too. Pay particular attention to the date on which the source was written.

SOURCE 1

From the work contract signed by all miners in the Olyokma region of Siberia, including those who worked in the Lena Goldfields from 1911 to 1912.

We undertake to fulfil in good faith any mining work at the Lenzoloto mines or wherever the administration sends us. In no case, may we refuse the work assigned us or change it on our own for tasks.

From 1 April until 1 October, the workday must consist of 11.5 working hours and from 1 October until 1 April, 11 hours. Lunch breaks are scheduled by the administration and are not included in the workday.

In winter … we will receive days off as required by law. During the summer, the administration will assign days off at least twice a month.

Before the end of the work contract, none of us has the right to ask to quit work. The administration has the right to fire us for the following reasons: (a) incompetent work, (b) absence from work three days in a row without appropriate cause, (c) laziness, (d) foolish behaviour, (e) contraction of an infectious disease, (f) for gathering crowds threatening to order and quiet, and (g) for any violation of the work contract on our part.

SOURCE 2

From *'Our Demands'*, a document sent to the managers of the Lenzoloto mines on 2 March 1912, at the beginning of the strike at the Lena Goldfields.

We demand:

The Expansion of living quarters for (a) sufficient air, (b) free lighting; (c) unmarried people should have one room for two people; (d) families should have one room.

Eight-hour workday; on holiday eves, seven hours; on Sundays and holidays work is not obligatory; overtime work must be paid at a higher rate.

Every day's work should be entered into a table and totalled every month; the tables should be available to workers on a daily basis.

Medical aid should be provided at first request; during illness caused by Lenzoloto, pay must occur at the normal rate and for other illnesses, at one-half pay.

The administration cannot fire on the basis of caprice but only with agreement of a workers' commission.

No forced women's labour.

Food should be issued to workers on the same conditions as for managers; all food products should be issued in the presence of a worker deputy.

Managers must address workers politely.

The impact of the First World War

On the eve of the First World War Russia's army was superficially impressive. However, at a deeper level, it had serious weaknesses.

The army's strengths

The Russian army was the largest in Europe, numbering 1.4 million soldiers and 3 million **reservists**.

Military reforms in 1908 were based on a comprehensive ten-year programme to modernise the army, including the introduction of military aircraft.

In 1913 the Minister of War Vladimir Sukhomlinov adopted the 'Grand Plan'. The new plan was a response to increased tensions in the Balkans. The plan proposed an offensive strategy in order to secure Russia's western borders.

Problems in the army

Long-term problems included the following:
● Incompetent generals who had senior positions due to their family connections, not their ability to lead.
● Russian soldiers were the least educated of any European army.
● Russian industry was still undeveloped relative to other European nations, therefore Russian arms production was comparatively inefficient.

Additionally, military reform was not entirely effective:
● Modernisation plans were designed to ensure the army was ready for war in 1917; therefore the army was not ready for the outbreak of war in 1914.
● The Tsar authorised a massive programme of naval expansion in 1907 which took up a large part of the military budget. However, as Russia faced no major threats from other naval powers this did almost nothing to defend the nation.

The course of the First World War

The First World War exposed the weaknesses of the Russian army. Initial victories were short-lived. Russian defeat at the Battle of Tannenberg led to the 'Great Retreat' of 1915. Attempts to regain the initiative through the 'Brusilov Offensive' of 1916 also ended in failure.

Economic problems including inflation and supplies for cities

The First World War led to catastrophic economic consequences for Russia.

Inflation and food shortages

Growing inflation was a major problem during the First World War. Inflation had a major impact on food prices. By 1917, inflation had reached 200 per cent. Food prices went up even faster. The price of flour, for example, rose by 500 per cent.

By January 1917 Petrograd was receiving only 48 per cent of its total grain requirements. The army was also forced to reduce rations from 4,000 to 2,000 calories a day.

Urbanisation

The growth of the war economy meant more workers were employed in factories in the cities. Between 1914 and 1917, Petrograd's population rose from 2.1 to 2.7 million.

Munitions crisis

Russia's military planners had assumed that modern wars would be relatively short. Therefore the army had not stockpiled enough weapons to keep fighting. Russian industry also lacked the capacity to produce sufficient quantities of munitions.

By mid-1915 the munitions crisis was so bad that Russian artillery units were limited to three shells per day. As a result, Russia experienced severe shortages of munitions in the spring of 1915, which led to military setbacks.

Transport crisis

Russia's transport networks struggled to cope with the need to transport troops, munitions and food. This exacerbated food shortages in the cities and munitions shortages on the front line.

St Petersburg, Petrograd, Leningrad

The capital city of Russia changed its name three times between 1894 and 1924. Originally called St Petersburg, the name was changed to Petrograd in 1914, because the government believed that St Petersburg sounded too Germanic. In 1924 the city was renamed Leningrad in honour of Lenin. The city changed its name back to St Petersburg in 1991.

(i) Develop the detail   a

Look at the following sample A-level exam question and a paragraph written in answer to this question. The paragraph contains a limited amount of detail. Annotate the paragraph to add additional detail to the answer.

'Russia was thoroughly modernised in the years 1906–14.' How far do you agree with this statement?

The military was one aspect of Russia that was only partially modernised in the years 1906–14. There were some attempts to modernise the army such as a new plan in 1908. However, the plan did not tackle some of the long-standing problems. Also by 1914 the plan had not fully taken effect. Finally, aspects of the plan were ineffective as they did not address Russia's real defence needs. Therefore, the Russian military was only partially modernised as the reforms that were introduced did not prepare Russia to fight a truly modern war in 1914.

(i) You're the examiner   a

Look at the following sample A-level exam question and a paragraph written in answer to this question. Read the paragraph and the mark scheme provided on page 90. Decide which level you would award the paragraph. Write the level below, along with a justification for your choice.

'Russia was thoroughly modernised in the years 1906–14.' How far do you agree with this statement?

Another aspect of Russia that was not fully modernised was the army. Russian industry lagged behind the rest of Europe so arms production was inefficient. Modernisation plans had been designed to upgrade the army by 1917, but the war broke out in 1914. Also soldiers were the least educated in Europe.

Level:

Mark:

Reason for choosing this level and this mark:

_____

_____

The impact of the First World War: political problems

The war led to major changes in Russian politics. In the short term the vast majority of Russians united in a patriotic desire to win the war. However, by 1915, military defeat, economic failure and rumours about the royal family led to demands for reform.

Nicholas, Alexandra and Rasputin

In August 1915, Russian armies retreated from Russian Poland. As a result of this disaster, the Tsar became commander-in-chief of the army.

With the Tsar on the front line, rumours circulated that the Tsarina Alexandra was running the government. This undermined faith in the government:

- The Tsarina had been born in Germany. Rumours circulated that she was a German agent. Indeed, during this period Boris Sturmer, a Russian citizen of German descent, was appointed head of government.
- Rumours also suggested that the Tsar and Tsarina were under the influence of Grigori Rasputin. These rumours were damaging as Rasputin had a reputation as a drunk and a womaniser. Indeed, there were rumours that Rasputin was sleeping with the Tsarina and the Princesses.

Ministerial leapfrog

From the beginning of 1916 government ministers were appointed and sacked with increasing frequency. This 'ministerial leapfrog' was blamed on the Tsarina and Rasputin, who were accused of giving jobs to their favourites.

The murder of Rasputin

In December 1916 Prince Felix Yusupov, working with other aristocrats and politicians, assassinated Rasputin, in order to stop rumours of scandal. However, the murder of Rasputin failed to change public opinion.

Zemgor

Zemgor was an organisation that co-ordinated voluntary support for the war effort. Zemgor comprised the Zemstvo Union, and the Union of Towns which represented local government across the country. Its work included:

- production of uniforms, medicine and munitions
- distribution of food
- aid to refugees
- medical care
- organising military detachments: the **Zemstvo Hussars**.

Headed by **Prince Lvov**, a member of the Kadets, Zemgor was efficient and well organised. However, its resources were limited. Therefore, the organisation contributed only five per cent of the resources necessary to support the war effort.

Zemgor's effectiveness compared favourably to the inefficiencies of the government's own wartime organisation.

The Progressive Bloc

The Progressive Bloc was a political alliance of Duma deputies, united by their desire for constitutional reform.

As the Russian army was forced into the 'Great Retreat' of 1915, in part due to the munitions crisis, pressure mounted on the Tsar to recall the Duma. In the summer of 1915 the Tsar recalled the Duma. The majority of Duma deputies, 236 of the 442, formed the Progressive Bloc. They demanded a 'government of confidence': a new government comprising leading members of the Duma, which could manage the war effort competently.

The Tsar's response

The Tsar refused to collaborate with the Progressive Bloc and Zemgor. Nicholas believed that the Duma had no right to play a role in government. The Tsar dismissed the Duma in September 1915, less than a month since it had reassembled. Some within government also believed that Zemgor was a front for revolutionaries. Nicholas II's refusal to work with the Duma and the Zemgor weakened Russia's ability to organise the war effort.

Withdrawal from government

As the economy worsened, and there was no sign of military breakthrough, the Tsar became increasingly unpopular. Even Duma moderates were critical of the Tsar, when the Fourth Duma reassembled in February 1916.

The Tsar responded by withdrawing from government. He relocated to his military headquarters in Stavka, and relied on incompetent and unpopular ministers to supervise the civilian population and the economy.

Spot the inference   **a**

High-level answers avoid excessive summarising or paraphrasing the sources. Instead they make inferences from the sources, as well as analysing their value in terms of their context.

> Why is Source 1 valuable to the historian for an enquiry into the government's attitude towards the Zemgor during the First World War?
>
> Explain your answer using the source, the information given about it and your own knowledge of the historical context. **AS**

Below are a source and a series of statements. Read the source and decide which of the statements:

- make inferences from the source (I)
- paraphrase the source (P)
- summarise the source (S)
- cannot be justified from the source (X).

Fill in the boxes below with either I, P, S or X:

- The Duma was elected by the Russian people. ☐

- The government's attitude to the Zemgor was inexplicable. The Zemgor did some good work, but spent too much money, and Prince Lvov would have been made to pay for his anarchist principles if the revolution had not happened. ☐

- The Zemgor was better funded than official government departments. ☐

- The author of Source 1 believes that the government had a contradictory attitude to the Zemgor, as it both gave the Zemgor money and distrusted it. ☐

- The author of Source 1 believes that the Zemgor had revolutionary intentions prior to the February Revolution. ☐

SOURCE 1

From the memoirs of Vladimir Gurko, written in the 1920s. Gurko was a member of the State Council which advised the Tsar. He was also sympathetic to extreme right-wing political groups who opposed reform in Russia.

The government's attitude towards the Zemgor was incomprehensible. On the one hand, it treated the Zemgor with utter, complete and sometimes open distrust. On the other, it supplied it with tens of millions of rubles and exercised almost no control over how this was spent. According to a government report every private soldier at the front knew that the government never had anything the soldiers needed, while the Zemgor had everything. In the final analysis the spending of the Zemgor was never once efficiently checked by any government agency.

But the Zemgor was something more than a body which included a multitude of revolutionary agitators and many who desired to avoid active military service. Zemgor detachments (the famous Zemgor Hussars) working at the front were well equipped. The Zemgor did some good work, and to its credit, it did not engage in open revolutionary activity until the February Revolution.

Had the war not ended in revolution, the heads of the Zemgor would have been called to account. Prince Lvov enlisted renowned agitators in the organisation. But he did this, not to create well-organised propaganda, but because his motto was to let all persons do as they wished. These anarchist principles were later demonstrated to the full, and Russia paid for them dearly.

The February Revolution

By the end of 1916 the war had created extreme economic hardship across Russia. This led to the growth of unrest in towns and the countryside.

Urban unrest

Strikes and protests began to occur in major cities such as Moscow and Petrograd. As the war went on goods became increasingly scarce. With inflation growing, the value of wages of industrial workers was cut by half in 1916. Even in Petrograd, which had received a large amount of investment during the war, wages were still on average 20 per cent lower in **real terms** than they had been in 1914.

As millions of refugees fled from the fighting, they arrived in large numbers in Russia's already crowded cities, placing a great deal of strain on the facilities in urban areas.

Strikes increased as the war continued:

Year	Workers on strike
1914 (Sept–Dec)	10,000
1915	540,000
1916	880,000

Unrest in the country

The war caused great hardship in rural areas, which by 1916 led to widespread protest. Young male peasants were conscripted in large numbers. Consequently, there was a dramatic drop in the rural workforce. Horses were also **requisitioned** in order to help with war work. Grain prices were kept low and, with rising inflation, standards of living for many in the countryside fell.

The Tsar's response

The Okhrana and the leadership of the army were well aware of unrest in the country and the city. The Tsar, however, was complacent. Based on the experience of 1905, he assumed that his government could survive even large-scale unrest.

International Women's Day

In February the government announced that bread would be rationed from 1 March. This led to panic buying, food shortages and more strikes. On 23 February thousands of women took to the streets of Petrograd to celebrate International Women's Day. Female workers in Petrograd's major textile factories went on strike in protest at bread rationing and appealed to male workers at the Putilov Engineering Works to join the strike.

General strike in Petrograd

In the last days of February the Tsar's hold on power crumbled. By 25 February 200,000 people were protesting on the streets of Petrograd. The workers established Soviets to put forward their demands. **Cossack** troops, who had been instructed to suppress the protests, refused to put down the rebellion. Indeed, reports reached the Tsar that his own troops were handing out rifles and bread to the people of Petrograd.

Mind map

Use the information on the opposite page to add detail to the mind map below on the causes of the February Revolution.

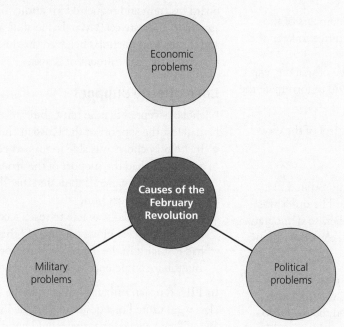

 Simple essay style

Below is a sample exam question. Use your own knowledge and the information on the opposite page to produce a plan for this question. Choose four general points, and provide three pieces of specific information to support each general point. Once you have planned your essay, write the introduction and conclusion for the essay. The introduction should list the points to be discussed in the essay. The conclusion should summarise the key points and justify which point was the most important.

How accurate is it to say that the principal reasons for urban and rural unrest in 1916 were economic?

The Provisional Committee and the Petrograd Soviet

By late February the Tsar's government effectively lost control of the capital. On 27 February, two new organisations were formed:

- The Provisional Committee – 12 members of the Duma formed an emergency committee to keep the government going during the crisis.
- The Petrograd Soviet – a committee of workers was formed to co-ordinate the strikes and to formulate the demands of the workers.

These two groups effectively took control of the city.

Order Number 1

On 1 March the Petrograd Soviet demonstrated its authority by issuing Order Number 1. The order was directed at the army. It instructed soldiers to democratise the army. It gave soldiers the power to elect their own officers and to question orders.

Although the order had no legal authority, the majority of the Russian army obeyed it. In this way the order was significant because it demonstrated the *de facto* authority of the Duma and ended the authority of Tsar and his generals over the army.

The actions of the Provisional Committee

Key members of the Duma convinced important generals that military intervention could ignite a **Civil War**. Consequently, in the last days of February the Russian army did not attempt to put down the revolution in the capital.

Order Number 1 further weakened the Tsar's position. Rodzianko, one of the leading figures within the Duma, saw an opportunity to remove the Tsar. He encouraged General Nikolai Ruzsky, commander of the Northern Front, to meet the Tsar at Pskov and encourage him to resign.

The middle class and the Tsar

The Russian middle class were unwilling to support the Tsar. During 1915 factory owners in Petrograd had prospered due to profitable government contracts to produce munitions. However, middle-class Russians believed that the monarchy was corrupt and incompetent. They blamed the Tsar for the military and economic failures of 1915.

The middle class in Petrograd supported the new Provisional Committee hoping that it would lead to a more effective and democratic government.

The abdication of Nicholas II

Representatives from the Duma met with the Tsar on board his train and requested his **abdication**. The Tsar agreed to abdicate on 2 March. He abdicated for himself and for his son. Nicholas believed that his son was too ill to assume the government of Russia.

Loss of elite support

Nicholas accepted that he must abdicate as he recognised he had lost the support of the Russian elite:

- In 1905 Nicholas was able to reassert control of Russia because he had the support of the army. However, in 1917 senior generals indicated that they were not willing to support him.
- In 1905 Nicholas was able to reach a compromise with the middle class. However, in 1917 the middle class had lost faith in the Tsar, due to rumours of corruption and the incompetence of his wartime government.

In 1917, Russian military leaders and the Russian middle class were united in a desire to win the First World War. They believed that they could build on the limited success achieved in the Brusilov Offensive, and work through Zemgor to solve the munitions crisis. In this context, they believed that the Tsar was an obstacle to military success and economic efficiency. Therefore the Russian elite abandoned the Tsar in order to win the war.

Write the question

The following sources relate to the abdication of the Tsar. Having read the previous pages about the Tsar, write an exam-style question using the sources.

1 How far could the historian make use of Sources 1 and 2 together to investigate ...?

_____

_____

Explain your answer, using both sources, the information given about them and your own knowledge of the historical context.

2 Why is Source 2 valuable to the historian for an enquiry into ...?

_____

Explain your answer using the source, the information given about it and your own knowledge of the historical context. **AS**

SOURCE 1

From the Memoirs of Count Paul Benckendorff, Grand Marshall of the Russian Imperial Court under Tsar Nicholas II. Benckendorff was with Nicholas II in the last stages of his reign and was imprisoned with the royal family after Nicholas II's abdication. His memoirs of this period were published in 1927.

In the course of Sunday, February 27, 1917, the revolution, which for some days had raged in Petrograd, spread through the whole city. The troops, reserve battalions, ill-recruited and ill-led, had nearly all of them gone over to the side of the revolution. Towards evening only a few battalions remained faithful to the Emperor. These occupied the Winter Palace. The revolutionaries were victorious in the town.

Towards 10 o'clock in the evening, General Grooten, Assistant Commandant of the Palaces, came to tell me that the Minister of War, General Belyaev, had just telephoned. He reported that at a meeting of the Council of Ministers which had been held at the Palace, Rodzianko (President of the Duma) had warned the ministers that the Empress was in danger.

During the night of the 27th–28th February, General Khabalov [in command of the military district of Petrograd] telephoned. He told me that he was holding the Winter Palace with such troops as had remained faithful, that these troops were dying of hunger. I told him that there was very little food left in the palace, and that I would give orders for all that there was to be given to him. The despairing attitude of the General, the panic which was plain in all his words, proved to me that there was no more hope and that resistance could only last a few more hours.

SOURCE 2

Tsar Nicholas II's Abdication Proclamation, 2 March 1917.

In the days of the great struggle against the foreign enemies, who for nearly three years have tried to enslave our fatherland, the Lord God has been pleased to send down on Russia a new heavy trial.

Internal popular disturbances threaten to have a disastrous effect on the future conduct of this persistent war. The destiny of Russia, the honour of our heroic army, the welfare of the people, and the whole future of our dear fatherland demand that the war should be brought to a victorious conclusion whatever the cost.

The cruel enemy is making his last efforts. In these decisive days in the life of Russia, We thought it Our duty of conscience to help Our people in the speedy attainment of victory.

In agreement with the Imperial Duma We have thought it well to renounce the Throne of the Russian Empire and to lay down the supreme power. As We do not wish to part from Our beloved son, We transmit the succession to Our brother, the Grand Duke Michael Alexandrovich, and give Him Our blessing to mount the Throne of the Russian Empire.

In the name of Our dearly beloved homeland, We call on Our faithful sons of the fatherland to fulfil their sacred duty to the fatherland.

May the Lord God help Russia!

NICHOLAS II

Exam focus

Below is a high-level answer to an exam-style question. Read the essay and the comments around it.

How far did the fundamental features of Tsarist autocracy remain in the decade following the 1905 Revolution?

The 1905 Revolution led to some constitutional reform. Nonetheless, the fundamental features of Tsarist autocracy stayed in place to a considerable extent in the years 1905–15. Tsarism has several fundamental features, including the Tsar's sovereignty, the lack of democracy and individual rights, and the lack of civil society. Clearly, by 1915 the Tsar was still legal sovereign, and Russia cannot be called a democracy. However, individual rights, at least for the middle class, were beginning to be respected, and civil society was beginning to develop.

The Tsar's sovereignty remained in the decade following the 1905 Revolution. His sovereignty was reasserted in Article 4 of the Fundamental Laws, which were promulgated in April 1906. His sovereignty was also clear as he retained sole authority over command of the army and dealings with foreign nations. In spite of the introduction of a Duma in 1906, Article 87 of the Fundamental Laws stated that the Tsar still had 'supreme sovereign power'. This meant that Nicholas had the right to make laws without consultation with the Duma. Therefore in a *de jure* sense the Tsar retained sovereign power. However, following the 1905 Revolution the Tsar's powers were constrained. Following conflict with the first two Dumas the Tsar wanted to take away the Duma's law-making power and make it purely consultative. However, he was unable to do so, because he knew that there would be protest from the Kadets and the Octoberists. Therefore, although the Tsar retained *de jure* sovereignty there were *de facto* constraints on his power and in this sense his sovereignty was not as secure as it had been before 1905.

Lack of democracy also continued to be a feature of the Tsarist autocracy in the decade following 1905. The first two Dumas introduced a degree of democracy as they genuinely represented all Russian men. However, following Stolypin's electoral law of 1906 the upper and middle class were massively over-represented, and therefore the Duma was considerably less democratic. Even the first two Dumas were not truly democratic as they did not represent women, and as they had no power to introduce popular reform. This was clear from the way in which the Tsar dismissed both of them. The Fourth Duma, which was elected in 1912 and served until the fall of the Tsar in 1917, was clearly not democratic as it was dominated by the middle class, and as it was unable to force through popular reforms. In this way, it is evident that the fundamentally undemocratic nature of Tsarism remained as at no point in the decade following 1905 did the reforms establish genuine people power.

However, there were steps forward in terms of individual rights, at least for the middle class. The rights promised in the Fundamental Laws were quickly taken away by Stolypin's state of emergency. Indeed, government repression against Russia's workers was clear in events such as the Lena Goldfields massacre. However, the middle class were more fortunate. For example, Guchkov, leader of the Octoberists was critical of the Tsar's government, and remained free from persecution. Moreover, by 1914 Russia had a largely free press, which published criticisms of the Tsar. Clearly, although the majority of Russians still had no legal rights, there were some changes in the fundamental features of government because of the emergence of a free press and because of greater respect of the political rights of the liberal middle class.

Excellent focus on the question.

The essay opens by defining the fundamental features of Tsarist autocracy.

The essay is structured around the fundamental features of Tsarist autocracy set out in the introduction.

The essay considers aspects of sovereignty that stayed the same and aspects that changed.

The essay deploys well-selected knowledge to support its points.

Perhaps the biggest change to the fundamental features of Tsarism was the emergence of civil society. Traditionally, Tsarism had made independent groups such as political parties and unions illegal. This changed in 1906. Following 1906 multiple political parties were established, and unionisation of the working class increased. As a result, the number of workers on strike increased from 750,000 to almost 1.5 million in the first half of 1914. Tsarism continued to interfere with independent groups. Radical parties were infiltrated by the Okhrana, and all of the Duma Deputies involved in the Vyborg protests were punished. However, the Kadets, Octoberists and numerous unions grew. Therefore, the emergence of civil society shows that one of the fundamental features of Tsarism changed because the legal existence of independent groups allowed people to have some independence from the Tsar's government.

In conclusion the fundamental features of Tsarist autocracy continued in the decade after the 1905 Revolution, as the Tsar's sovereignty remained largely intact and because government barely became any more democratic. Nonetheless, reforms did allow civil society to grow, at least for the middle class, and therefore the fundamental features of Tsarist autocracy did not remain wholly intact in the decade following the 1905 Revolution.

The essay concludes with a supported judgement based on the criteria established in the opening of the essay.

This is a strong answer because it focuses clearly on the question, it analyses the key features of Tsarist autocracy, and it deploys accurate and relevant knowledge to reach a substantiated judgement.

Reverse engineering

The best essays are based on careful plans. Read the essay and the comments and try to work out the general points of the plan used to write the essay. Once you have done this, note down the specific examples used to support each general point.

AS Level questions

1 How far did the 1905 Revolution change the government of Russia, in the period 1894–1914?

2 Were the Tsar's weaknesses the main reason for the February Revolution of 1917?

3 To what extent did the Russian economy change in the years 1894–1914?

4 How significant was the Okhrana in the survival of Tsarism in the years 1894–1905?

5 How far do you agree that Russia became a freer society in the years 1906–14?

Some more AS Level questions to try at the end of Section 4 (page 80)

1 To what extent was the leadership of the Reds and the Whites responsible for the outcome of the Civil War?

2 How significant were changes in Communist economic policy in the consolidation of Communist power in the years 1918–24?

3 To what extent were there changes in Communist economic policy in the years 1918–24?

4 How far were the military weaknesses of the Communists' opponents responsible for Communist victory in the Civil War?

5 How widespread was opposition to the Communist government in the years 1918–21?

The nature of dual power

Nicholas II's abdication named his uncle Grand Duke Mikhail the new Tsar. Milyukov and right-wing members of the Kadets welcomed this outcome. However, the workers of Petrograd refused to support a constitutional monarchy.

The Grand Duke Mikhail abdicated on 3 March 1917. This decisively ended the power of the Romanovs. However, the February Revolution had failed to establish a legitimate new government. Rather, the overthrow of Tsarism led to a situation which Trotsky called Dual Power, in which the Petrograd Soviet and the **Provisional Government** shared power.

Dual power

Dual power was not a formal constitutional relationship. Indeed, the relationship between the two institutions changed over time.

The Petrograd Soviet and the Provisional Government had different kinds of authority, and saw themselves as having different roles:

- The Provisional Government claimed to be the sole legal government of Russia. However, its role was to govern temporarily, until a new constitution could be established by a democratically elected **Constituent Assembly**.
- The Petrograd Soviet was a democratically elected body representing the working people and soldiers of Petrograd. The Soviet did not claim to govern Russia. Nonetheless, it had the support of the vast majority of the capital's workers and soldiers. Therefore, it could control the local garrisons, the factories and the railways of Petrograd. In this sense, it was more powerful than the Provisional Government.

The political complexion of the Provisional Government

The First Provisional Government was dominated by former members of the Progressive Bloc. Prince Lvov, the head of Zemgor, was head of the First Provisional Government. Milyukov and other leading Kadets played leading roles. The government also included **Alexander Kerensky**, a socialist who had been elected to the Fourth Duma.

The power of the Provisional Government

The Provisional Government could not rely on the support of the army due to Soviet Order Number 1. Without overwhelming military power the Provisional Government was dependent on the Soviet to ensure that its measures were carried out.

Support for the Provisional Government

The Provisional Government had a difficult relationship with the people of Petrograd.

Early support

The threat of further rebellions forced the new government to guarantee basic rights including:
- freedom of expression and assembly
- freedom of conscience
- universal suffrage for all adults
- equal rights for minorities.

These measures, which were introduced in early March, won over the majority of the working people of Petrograd.

The role of radical parties

During March the Mensheviks, SRs and even the Bolsheviks offered a degree of support for the new government. Radical parties agreed that Russia needed a period of parliamentary democracy and capitalism before a truly socialist revolution.

Support from the Soviet

In March and April the Provisional Government and the Soviet were in agreement over major issues. Importantly, leading members of both institutions favoured 'revolutionary defencism': the policy of continuing to fight the First World War in order to defend the Revolution. Therefore the two organisations were able to collaborate successfully.

Spot the mistake

Look at the following sample exam question and a paragraph written in answer to this question. Why does this paragraph not get into Level 4? Once you have identified the mistake, rewrite the paragraph so that it displays the qualities of Level 4. The mark scheme on page 90 will help you.

How accurate is it to say that the Petrograd Soviet undermined the power of the Provisional Government consistently between March and October 1917?

The Petrograd Soviet undermined the power of the Provisional Government from the very beginning. The presence of two organisations representing different social classes created a situation which Trotsky called Dual Power. What is more the Petrograd Soviet's authority eclipsed that of the Provisional Government. The First Provisional Government was made up of unelected middle-class liberals. The Soviet, by contrast, was made up of workers and soldiers and was elected regularly. It had de facto control of the factories and railways of the city as well as the garrisons of troops in the capital.

Complete the paragraph

Look at the following sample exam question and a paragraph written in answer to this question. The paragraph contains a point and specific examples, but lacks a concluding analytical link back to the question. Complete the paragraph, adding this link in the space provided.

'The authority of the Provisional Government was challenged consistently in the period March to October 1917.' How far do you agree with this statement?

The authority of the Provisional Government was certainly challenged in the weeks immediately after the February Revolution. For example, 'Dual Power' and the nature of the Petrograd Soviet undermined the Provisional Government. The Petrograd Soviet had genuine authority as it was democratically elected. The Petrograd Soviet truly represented the workers of the Petrograd, whereas the First Provisional Government was not elected. What is more the First Provisional Government was dominated by middle-class liberals and aristocrats. Therefore the workers of Petrograd were loyal to the Petrograd Soviet to a much greater extent than they were to the Provisional Government. Therefore ...

_____

_____

The aims and membership of the Petrograd Soviet

The Soviet was established in late February 1917 in order to co-ordinate striking workers across Petrograd. In many ways it was similar to the St Petersburg Soviet of 1905:

- The Soviet was elected regularly and directly by factory workers and soldiers living in Petrograd.
- Delegates could be recalled by the factories or army units that elected them.
- Delegates received the same pay as ordinary workers.

However, unlike in 1905, in 1917 intellectuals could become full members of the Soviet.

The aims of the Soviet

The Soviet's aims were to defend the rights of the workers under the new 'bourgeois government'. In this sense they wanted a 'bourgeois government' which respected the rights of the working class.

The spread of Soviets

As the Tsar's government broke down Soviets emerged across Russia. The relationship between the Petrograd Soviet and the Provisional Government was replicated across the country. In each town the Soviet and the local government were forced to work together.

Congresses

The Soviets collaborated with each other. Indeed, in June 1917 representatives from Soviets across the whole of Russia met for the First All-Russian Congress of Soviets. Of the 1,090 delegates at the First Congress the majority were SRs and Mensheviks.

Lenin and the Soviets

From April 1917 Lenin argued that the Soviets should take over the government of Russia, replacing the undemocratic bourgeois Provisional Government. By late 1917 this view was extremely popular. Indeed, Lenin's book *State and Revolution* which was written late in 1917 won the Bolsheviks considerable support due to its vision of a new democratic Russia in which workers and peasants ruled themselves.

Early political reforms

March reforms guaranteed fundamental freedoms:

- Freedom of expression – including freedom of the press.
- Freedom of assembly – including the freedom to protest against the government.

They also introduced profound changes to the legal system:

- Equal political and legal rights were guaranteed for all people regardless of religion or ethnic or national background.

The reforms promised a truly democratic Russia:

- The new government promised universal suffrage for all adults, including women.

There were also radical changes to the nature of the state:
- The Okhrana was abolished.
- The death penalty was abolished.
- There was an amnesty for political prisoners, including people convicted for terrorism.

The reforms reflected a radical transformation of Russian government. The key features of the Tsarist system, including autocratic government and police repression, were swept away.

The limits of reform

The Petrograd Soviet pushed for greater reforms. A maximum eight-hour day was a long-standing demand of working people, and the peasants wanted land reform. However, the Provisional Government argued that reforms to work and reforms to property should wait until the Constituent Assembly was elected, as the Constituent Assembly would have a genuine mandate from the Russian people.

The impact of the reforms

The abolition of the political police and the guarantee of political rights meant that radical political leaders were free to return to Russia:
- **Joseph Stalin** arrived in Petrograd in March 1917.
- Lenin returned in April along with Grigori Zinoviev and Lev Kamenev.
- Nikolai Bukharin returned to Moscow in May.

Radicals from other political parties also returned, including Menshevik leaders Fyodor Dan and Julius Martov, and other Marxists such as **Felix Dzerzhinsky**.

The returning revolutionaries were also free to organise against the government. From March leading Bolsheviks campaigned against the continuation of the war, and from April leading Bolsheviks campaigned for a second revolution. In this sense early political reforms helped to destabilise the new government.

Explain the difference

The following sources give different accounts of the problems facing the Tsarist system during the First World War. List the ways in which the sources differ. Explain the differences between the sources using the provenance of the sources, and the historical context. The provenance appears at the top of the source. Make sure you stay focused on the differences that are relevant to the question.

How far could the historian make use of Sources 1 and 2 together to investigate the extent of support for the Provisional Government in March 1917? Explain your answer, using both sources, the information given about them and your own knowledge of the historical context.

Sources 1 and 2 imply different levels of support for the Provisional Government in March 1917 because ...

_____

_____

SOURCE 1

From an article written in *Pravda* by Joseph Stalin, 16 March 1917.

The other day General Kornilov informed the Petrograd Soviet that the Germans were planning an offensive against Russia. Rodzyanko and Guchkov took advantage of the opportunity to appeal to the army and the people to prepare to fight the war to a finish.

What, then, is the solution?

The solution is to bring pressure on the Provisional Government to make it declare its consent to start peace negotiations immediately.

The workers, soldiers and peasants must arrange meetings and demonstrations and demand that the Provisional Government shall come out openly and publicly in an effort to induce all the belligerent powers to start peace negotiations immediately, on the basis of recognition of the right of nations to self-determination.

Only then will the slogan 'Down with the war!' not run the risk of being transformed into empty and meaningless pacifism.

SOURCE 2

From an interview with the press given by Prince Lvov on 8 March 1917.

According to the information received by the Government, the liberation of the people is greeted with great joy, and everywhere the population meets the establishment of the new government halfway. At first we had apprehensions regarding the front, where soldiers live in a different emotional climate. But the troops recognise the new government.

Our essential task is the preparation for the Constituent Assembly, in which all the people and the troops must participate. Fortunately the public has become aware of the concept of the Constituent Assembly. Although a period of three to six months will be required for preparation.

Opposition to the Provisional Government

The continuation of the First World War was one of the first major issues that led to opposition to the Provisional Government.

Conflicting attitudes to the war

In essence, there were three main points of view on the war:

- Liberals wanted to continue the war to ensure Russian victory. Milyukov's appointment as Foreign Minister and Guchkov's appointment as Minister for War clearly demonstrated the First Provisional Government's commitment to fighting the war to a victorious conclusion.
- From 1914 to 1918 Bolsheviks and some SRs consistently argued for the war to end. For Lenin the First World War was an imperialist war, which sacrificed the lives of working people in order to provide more land and resources to make capitalists rich. In 1917 the Bolsheviks campaigned for a 'democratic peace'.
- The majority of the Mensheviks adopted a policy known as 'revolutionary defencism'. The policy was first worked out by the Georgian Menshevik Irakli Tsereteli. He argued that workers had a duty to continue fighting in order to defend their revolution.

From March 'revolutionary defencism' became the dominant view among SRs and Mensheviks.

The Milyukov crisis

The Milyukov crisis was the first major test of the relationship between the Provisional Government and the Petrograd Soviet.

In April, the Provisional Government and the Petrograd Soviet reached an agreement on the aims of the war. The 'Declaration of War Aims' committed the new government to 'revolutionary defencism'. However, it allowed Milyukov to restructure the war economy and aim for victory.

Milyukov's fall

Milyukov believed that 'revolutionary defencism' was a feeble policy which failed to take advantage of the opportunity to win the war that the fall of the Tsar had created.

On 18 April, Milyukov sent a telegram to Britain and France which committed Russia to fighting in order to achieve a 'decisive victory'.

Protest

The telegram was a betrayal of the compromise set out in the 'Declaration of War Aims'. Consequently, when the telegram was made public, soldiers and workers began protest marches demanding Milyukov's resignation. The Bolsheviks went further, demanding the overthrow of the Provisional Government.

The consequences of the crisis

Milyukov resigned on 2 May. However, his telegram had seriously undermined faith in the honesty of the new government.

In order to re-establish trust between the Provisional Government and the Soviet, Prince Lvov invited six of the leading members of the Soviet to join the government. Tsereteli, the architect of 'revolutionary defencism', was one of the six socialists to join the new cabinet.

Impact on the Mensheviks and SRs

Rather than strengthening the government, the decision of some Mensheviks and SRs to join the government undermined the authority of the moderate socialist parties. Following May, increasing numbers of workers and soldiers lost faith in the Mensheviks and SRs as they believed that they had entered an alliance with an untrustworthy capitalist dominated government.

The significance of the debate on the war

The debate on the war had a genuine political significance. First, it split the SRs and the Mensheviks between those who favoured ending the war and those who advocated 'revolutionary defencism'.

Second, as the war dragged on it created greater economic chaos and hardship for working people. Therefore, over the course of 1917 the Bolsheviks became increasingly popular as they alone were united in their desire for peace.

Select the detail

Below is a sample A-level exam question with the accompanying sources. Having read the question and the sources, complete the following activity.

How far could the historian make use of Sources 1 and 2 together to investigate the disagreements over the role of the Soviets in 1917?

Below are three claims that you could make when answering the question. Read the claims and then select quotes from the sources to support them. Remember to keep the quotes short, never copy more than a sentence.

1 Source 1 reflects the Menshevik view that 1917 was not the right time for a working-class revolution...

2 Source 2 has a more radical view of the role of the Soviet than Source 1; it argues...

3 Source 2 clearly shows that Lenin disagreed with Tsereteli, the author of Source 1, about the nature of the Soviet...

SOURCE 1

From a speech made by Irakli Tsereteli to the Petrograd Soviet in March 1917. Tsereteli was a Menshevik and a leading member of the Petrograd Soviet from March 1917 until May 1918. He was one of the members of the Soviet who first proposed the doctrine of 'revolutionary defencism' and served in the Provisional Government as Minister of Post and Telegraph from May to August 1917.

You weighed the situation from the point of view of the interest of the Russian people. You understood that the moment had not yet come to realise the socialist revolution: the ultimate task of the proletariat, a task which has not been realised in other more advanced nations. You understood that this was the hour for a complete victory of bourgeois democracy, a victory in which the working class and all classes of the country were interested. You understood that the revolution just accomplished is a bourgeois revolution. You gave the bourgeoisie power, but at the same time you remained on guard to protect the newly gained freedom. The Soviet is responsible for supervision over the actions of the bourgeoisie. The Soviet is the dependable, steadfast stronghold of freedom, but other classes are also interested in this freedom. And if in the period of revolution, comrades, the power will not be supported by the whole Russian people, the dark forces might deal the revolution a blow. We must be able to organise the Soviet so that it can supervise the bourgeoisie and at the same time support with all of its authority the policies of the Provisional Government.

SOURCE 2

From Lenin's April Theses presented to meetings of the Bolsheviks and the Mensheviks on 4 April 1917.

No support for the Provisional Government; the utter falsity of all its promises should be made clear, particularly of those relating to the renunciation of annexations.

Recognition of the fact that in most of the Soviets of Workers' Deputies our Party is in a minority, so far a small minority, as against a bloc of all the petty-bourgeois opportunist elements, from the Popular Socialists and the Socialist-Revolutionaries down to the Organising Committee (Chkheidze, Tsereteli, etc.), Steklov, etc., etc., who have yielded to the influence of the bourgeoisie and spread that influence among the proletariat.

The masses must be made to see that the Soviets of Workers' Deputies are the *only possible* form of revolutionary government, and that therefore our task is, as long as *this* government yields to the influence of the bourgeoisie, to present a patient, systematic, and persistent explanation of the errors of their tactics, an *explanation* especially adapted to the practical needs of the masses.

It is not our *immediate* task to 'introduce' socialism, but only to bring social production and the distribution of products at once under the *control* of the Soviets of Workers' Deputies.

Opposition to the Provisional Government, April to July

From April to July support for the Provisional Government deteriorated.

Lenin's return and the April Theses

Lenin's return to Russia in April 1917 was a turning point in attitudes towards the Provisional Government. In March all of the major Marxist and socialist parties in Russia had accepted that Russia was not ready for a socialist revolution. Lenin rejected this consensus, arguing that a socialist revolution in Russia was essential.

As soon as Lenin arrived in Petrograd he set out his April Theses. The Theses contained three major slogans which appealed to the majority of Russians:

- Peace – appealed to war-weary soldiers and workers and peasants who had suffered due to the war.
- Land – appealed to Russian peasants who wanted the revolution to lead to land reform, and who, over time, had become frustrated at the Provisional Government's refusal to redistribute land.
- Bread – promised an end to the hardship of the war.

Lenin also argued for 'all power to the Soviets'. As workers and peasants trusted the Soviets more than the Provisional Government, this slogan also became increasingly popular.

Lenin's impact

Initially Lenin's return had little impact. Marxists such as Tsereteli who had been in Petrograd since mid-March believed that Lenin was simply out of touch with the situation in Russia. Some Mensheviks even claimed that Lenin's Theses indicated that he had gone mad.

Nonetheless, Lenin's April Theses attracted the support of some revolutionaries such as Trotsky who had previously opposed the Bolsheviks.

The June Offensive

Following the resignation of Milyukov, Alexander Kerensky was appointed Minister of War. Kerensky was determined to help bring about an Allied victory, and to restore the authority of the Provisional Government. Therefore, he launched the June Offensive.

Kerensky toured the front line encouraging soldiers to support the new attack. However, the attack was a disaster. German reinforcements strengthened the Austro-Hungarian troops. Moreover, 48 Russian battalions refused to fight. Over 150,000 Russian soldiers lost their lives and even more deserted the front line.

The consequences of the offensive

The ill-fated offensive weakened the Provisional Government. The military disaster made the Provisional Government look weak and ineffective. What is more, there was criticism of the way in which a bourgeois government had sent workers and peasants to their deaths, while factory owners and landowners stayed safely out of the fighting.

The June Offensive also weakened the Mensheviks and SRs. The Mensheviks and SRs had joined the government in May promising to work to bring about peace. However, they immediately became involved planning the new offensive. This made the moderate socialists look like hypocrites.

The July Days

Military defeat and disillusionment with the Provisional Government led to a new political crisis. On 3 July, Kadet ministers resigned from the government. This provoked a military uprising.

Around 70,000 soldiers and armed workers surrounded the Tauride Palace in Petrograd, which housed both the Provisional Government and the Petrograd Soviet. The protestors, supported by the Bolsheviks, demanded that the Petrograd Soviet seize power.

However, the leaders of the Soviet refused. Lenin also backed down once the Provisional Government sent troops to resist the uprising. Government forces tried to disperse the armed protestors, leading to two days of riots.

The impact of the July Days

Leaders of the Provisional Government denounced the Bolsheviks as a threat to the stability of Russia.

On 6 July soldiers surrounded the Bolshevik Headquarters at Kshesinskaia Mansion and 500 Bolsheviks inside surrendered. The government started a propaganda campaign accusing Lenin of being a German spy. Lenin fled to Finland in order to escape arrest. For the time being, it seemed that the Provisional Government was secure and the Bolsheviks had failed.

Establish criteria

Below is a sample exam question which requires you to make a judgement. The key term in the question has been underlined. Defining the meaning of the key term can help you establish criteria that you can use to make a judgement.

Read the question, define the key term and then set out two or three criteria based on the key term, which you can use to reach and justify a judgement.

'The authority of the Provisional Government was only <u>seriously undermined</u> after the failure of the June Offensive.' How far do you agree with this statement?

Definition:

_____

_____

Criteria to judge the extent to which the authority of the Provisional Government was only <u>seriously undermined</u> after the failure of the June Offensive:

_____

_____

Tip: what is the difference between undermining the authority of the Provisional Government and <u>seriously</u> undermining the authority of the Provisional Government?

How significant was the June Offensive in undermining the authority of the Provisional Government in the period March to October 1917? **AS**

Support your judgement

Below is a sample exam question and two basic judgements. Read the exam question and the two judgements. Support the judgement that you agree with most strongly by adding a reason that justifies the judgement.

'The authority of the Provisional Government was only seriously undermined after the failure of the June Offensive.' How far do you agree with this statement?

Prior to the failure of the June Offensive the authority of the Provisional Government had been damaged but it had never been seriously undermined …

_____

_____

The June Offensive clearly undermined the authority of the Provisional Government. However, the authority of the Provisional Government had already been seriously undermined, therefore …

_____

_____

Tip: whichever option you choose you will have to weigh up both sides of the argument. You could use words such as 'whereas' and 'although' in order to help the process of evaluation.

The second Provisional Government, July–October

The July Days had threatened to overthrow the government. Prince Lvov resigned, and Kerensky responded by forming a 'government of salvation of the revolution'. This second Provisional Government was based on a new coalition between moderate socialists and the Kadets.

Kerensky as prime minister

Kerensky had many strengths, and his appointment as head of government persuaded many Bolsheviks that they were beaten. Kerensky was a charismatic leader and a gifted orator. According to contemporary reports he was adept at winning the support of women.

He understood the importance of propaganda and therefore had his public appearances filmed, and played in cinemas. He also understood the importance of patriotism.

Kerensky was also a skilful politician. He cultivated good relationships with Mensheviks and liberals in order to ensure that his government worked harmoniously. Moreover, before the Revolution Kerensky was a lawyer who specialised in defending revolutionaries. Therefore, he knew many of the leaders of the Soviet.

Kerensky's weaknesses

Kerensky had very little administrative experience prior to forming his first government. Therefore he did not fully understand how to run the government.

Kerensky was also addicted to cocaine and morphine, which he used to help cope with the pressures of his role in government.

Kerensky's policies

Kerensky wanted to restore domestic order. Therefore he imposed repression, including:
- press censorship
- the establishment of military courts to punish deserters and Bolsheviks who were spreading anti-war propaganda in the army
- the death penalty for insubordination in the army.

Kerensky also promised more effective and efficient grain distribution to ensure that urban workers had food to eat. However, he was unable to persuade the peasants to trade their grain, as he refused to raise the price the government would pay. Consequently, his policy failed: the amount of bread available in Petrograd in late 1917 was just over half of the amount that had been available a year earlier.

Following the failure of the June Offensive Kerensky abandoned plans to launch new military campaigns and the Russian army disintegrated due to mass desertions. Austrian and German forces launched new attacks on Russian territory, capturing Riga, the capital of Latvia, in August. This caused panic that Russia's enemies were preparing to conquer Petrograd.

The membership of the new government

Kerensky became head of government at a time of crisis. Many socialists had lost faith in the government and Kadet leaders refused to serve in a socialist-led government. Therefore Kerensky struggled to assemble a coalition.

Kerensky's cabinet contained three Kadets. The majority of Kadets had abandoned liberalism, believing that Russia needed a military dictatorship. The Kadets in the cabinet did not represent the mainstream of the party and therefore did not win the government the support of the majority of Kadets.

Kerensky's cabinet also contained SRs and Mensheviks; however, these parties were also split. Moreover, the SRs and the Mensheviks were suspicious of the Kadets, which made holding the government together difficult.

Socialist factions

By July the Mensheviks and the SRs were split. In each case the right-wing **factions** favoured revolutionary defencism, and support for the Provisional Government. However, the left-wing factions favoured policies such as Soviet power, workers' control of industry and a **separate peace** to end the war with Germany.

Add the context

Below is a sample A-level exam question with the accompanying sources. Having read the question and the sources, complete the following activity.

How far could the historian make use of Sources 1 and 2 together to investigate the extent of popular support for Russian involvement in the First World War during 1917?

First, look for aspects of the source that refer to the events and discussion that were going on around the time that the source was written. Underline the key phrases and write a brief description of the context in the margin next to the source. Draw an arrow from the key phrase to the context. Try to find three key phrases in each source.

Tip: look at the information above the source – you should contextualise this too. Pay particular attention to the date on which the source was written.

SOURCE 1

From *'War Aims of Provisional Government'* published by the Provisional Government on 19 April 1917.

CITIZENS: The Provisional Government, having considered the military situation of the Russian State, and being conscious of its duty to the country, has resolved to tell the people directly and openly the whole truth.

The overthrown government has left the defence of the country in an utterly disorganised condition. By its criminal inactivity and inefficient methods, it disorganised our finances, food supply, transportation, and the supply of the army. It has undermined our economic organisation.

The Provisional Government, with the active and vigorous assistance of the whole nation, will make every effort to remove the dire consequences of the old regime. But time does not wait. The blood of large numbers of the sons of our fatherland has been flowing without limit during these two and a half years of war, and still the country remains exposed to the blows of a powerful enemy, who has seized entire provinces of our country, and is now, in the days of the birth of Russian freedom, menacing us with a new, determined assault.

The defence of our own inheritance by every means, and the liberation of our country from the invading enemy, constitute the foremost and most urgent task of our fighters, defending the nation's liberty.

SOURCE 2

From an article published in *The Cause of the People,* a Socialist Revolutionary newspaper published in Petrograd. The article was published on 23 August 1917.

The grave news from the Riga front tears the mind and the heart to pieces. How will Russia, the new people's Russia, respond to the news? Will Russia stir her energy, arousing a spontaneous desire for action, which unites everybody in the urge to resist? Or will Russia react to it as to the funeral of the motherland and the death of the revolution, helplessly dropping her hands?

News from the Riga front, sinister as it may be, still leaves some hope for salvation. Our troops fought heroically, defending their positions. There were no instances of wilful mass desertion as there were in earlier battles. Some units, according to newspaper reports, counterattacked under heavy fire, their banners flying, and singing revolutionary songs. Our retreat in Riga was not due to faint-heartedness and cowardice. It was due to the overwhelming superiority of the enemy's artillery.

The fate of the revolution is now being decided at the front. The Russian revolution could have killed the war, had our people understood the intimate connection between a victorious defence and freedom. Then the Provisional Government would not have had to use repressive measures and curtail the freedoms we have won. But in our country Bolshevik doctrines of utopian internationalism have spread among our people extinguishing their will to fight.

Economic and political problems

The formation of Kerensky's government took place at a time of deepening economic crisis. Rather than leading to more efficient economic organisation, as the Kadets had hoped, the revolution had led to a breakdown of the existing system.

Problems in agriculture

Inflation, which had been an ongoing problem during the war, became worse in 1917. Russian paper money lost half its value in the second half of 1917. Consequently, many peasants refused to accept payment in paper money. This, coupled with huge problems in Russia's transport network, led to a significant fall in the amount of bread available in the cities. In October of 1917 the government was able to purchase only 56 per cent of the grain it had purchased a year earlier.

By mid-1917 the countryside was also experiencing a new revolution. Peasants refused to wait for a new government to authorise land reform. Rather, landless peasants seized land from landlords.

Problems in industry

Life in the cities deteriorated dramatically during 1917. Between January and June the production of fuel fell by more than a third. Factory production also dropped by 36 per cent.

In response to deteriorating conditions workers launched strikes. From February to October, 2.5 million workers went on strike. From July, workers went further, democratising their factories. Workers elected factory committees that took control of production and wages. In response managers of large factories and mines in the Urals and the Donbass closed their operations, locking workers out. As a result production fell further.

The Kornilov Affair

Kerensky appointed General **Lavr Kornilov** to take control of the Russian army. Kornilov had no sympathy for revolutionaries and was keen to assert the government's authority over the Soviets, trades unions and unruly peasants. Kerensky hoped that Kornilov's hardline approach would help restore order.

Kornilov took the position of commander-in-chief, but demanded the government implement harsh, repressive policies:
- Strikes were banned for the duration of the war – striking workers could be punished by death.
- Railway workers were placed under military control.
- Desertion from the army was punishable by death.

The Kornilov Revolt

The actual events of the Kornilov Revolt are not clear. Kornilov apparently demanded to place Petrograd under military control. Kerensky refused, knowing that the workers of Petrograd would resist. As a result Kerensky dismissed Kornilov as commander-in-chief.

Kornilov responded by ordering a detachment of troops to march on Petrograd. Kerensky assumed that Kornilov was attempting a military takeover.

Arming the Bolsheviks

Kerensky was forced to ask the Petrograd Soviet to defend the capital. He agreed to arm the **Red Guards**, a Bolshevik-dominated militia. This decision strengthened the Bolsheviks, as Trotsky was chairman of the Soviet, and by the end of August the Bolsheviks had a third of the seats in the Soviet in August 1917. What is more, Kerensky agreed to release Bolsheviks from prison so that they could defend the capital.

Kornilov defeated

The Bolsheviks played a key role in defeating Kornilov's forces:
- Trotsky ordered railway unions to prevent the train carrying Kornilov's troops from entering the city.
- Bolsheviks infiltrated Kornilov's troops and persuaded many to abandon the attack.

Consequences of the revolt

The Kornilov Affair seriously weakened the Provisional Government:
- The vast majority of Russian workers lost faith in the Provisional Government.
- Discipline within the Russian armed forces deteriorated even further.

Support for the Bolsheviks grew. They were credited with saving the revolution. By September the Bolsheviks had won majorities in the Moscow and Petrograd Soviets.

Develop the detail

Below is a sample A-level exam question and a paragraph written in answer to this question. The paragraph contains a limited amount of detail. Annotate the paragraph to add additional detail to the answer.

How accurate is it to say that Kerensky's political failings were primarily responsible for the downfall of the Provisional Government by October 1917?

Kerensky's political failings were clearly one reason for the downfall of the Provisional Government by October 1917. Kerensky was responsible for an important military defeat. This led to an uprising that almost overthrew the Provisional Government. Kerensky also undermined the government by introducing repressive measures. His appointment of a new army leader also backfired. Clearly, Kerensky's political failings were one reason for the downfall of the Provisional Government because his decisions tended to weaken support for the government.

Introducing an argument

Below are a sample exam question, a list of key points to be made in the essay, and a simple introduction and conclusion for the essay. Read the question, the plan and the introduction and conclusion. Rewrite the introduction and the conclusion in order to develop an argument.

How significant was the Kornilov Affair in the downfall of the Provisional Government?

Key points

- The Kornilov Affair weakened the Provisional Government and strengthened the Bolsheviks.

- Longer-term economic problems also led to the downfall of the Provisional Government.

- Ongoing military failure also undermined the Provisional Government.

- Political polarisation played a role in the downfall of the Provisional Government.

Introduction

There is some evidence that the Kornilov Affair was the most significant factor in bringing down the Provisional Government. However, there were other factors. Longer-term economic problems such as inflation and food shortages, ongoing military failures such as the June Offensive and the loss of Riga, and increasing political polarisation all played a role in the fall of the Provisional Government by October 1917.

Conclusion

In conclusion there were a series of significant factors that led to the downfall of the Provisional Government, including the Kornilov Affair, long-term economic problems, ongoing military failures, and increasing political polarisation.

The October Revolution

The Kornilov Affair and continuing economic crisis provided the Bolsheviks with an opportunity to overthrow Kerensky. Lenin played a decisive role in persuading the Bolsheviks to seize power.

Lenin's influence on the Central Committee

In August, the Provisional Government announced that elections would take place for a new Constituent Assembly in November. Lenin knew that the Socialist Revolutionaries would win, and that the Constituent Assembly would have a mandate to create a democratic government. Therefore, he was determined to seize power before the election of the Constituent Assembly in November.

Lenin secretly returned to Petrograd on 10 October in order to persuade the **Bolshevik Central Committee** to support an armed seizure of power in Petrograd.

Divisions in the Central Committee

Lenin's plan did not have the support of the whole Central Committee. In essence, Lenin wanted to seize power immediately prior to the Second All-Russia Congress of Soviets, hoping that the Congress of Soviets would authorise the creation of a Bolshevik government.

Trotsky argued that Bolshevik action should be authorised by the Congress of Soviets. Lenin rejected the plan, arguing that this would rob the Bolsheviks of the element of surprise.

The Second All-Russia Congress of Soviets

The Second All-Russia Congress of Soviets was due to meet in Petrograd at the end of October. It brought together representatives of workers, soldiers and peasants from across Russia. The First Congress (see page 48) had supported the Provisional Government. However, due to growing economic problems, military failure, the desire for land reform and the Kornilov Affair, Lenin anticipated the Second Congress would back a new government that was committed to radical change.

Zinoviev and Kamenev, usually two of Lenin's strongest supporters, opposed any uprising, arguing that the Bolsheviks should join a coalition government with radical Mensheviks and SRs.

In spite of bitter divisions on the Bolshevik Central Committee, Lenin persuaded the majority to back his plan. Trotsky was given the role of planning the uprising in detail.

Trotsky and the Military Revolutionary Committee

Trotsky played a key role in the October Revolution. Trotsky was chair of the Petrograd Soviet, therefore he could organise the uprising through the Soviet. In this sense, he could make the uprising look like the Soviet seizing power, rather than the Bolsheviks seizing power.

The Military Revolutionary Committee

The **Military Revolutionary Committee** (MRC) was crucial to Trotsky's plan. The MRC was formed by the Mensheviks after the Kornilov Affair. It was an armed group, organised along military lines, formed to protect Petrograd from an attempted military takeover.

By October the MRC was under Bolshevik control. Indeed, it was headed by Trotsky, Stalin and Felix Dzerzhinsky, who like Trotsky had joined the Bolsheviks in mid-1917.

Pretext for action

In mid-October, the Provisional Government announced that Petrograd's troops were being moved away from the city. The Soviet were horrified. The Soviet assumed that the news meant that troops loyal to the Soviet were being moved out of the city, so the government could take control of the Soviet.

Trotsky used fears about Kerensky's orders as a pretext to ready the MRC for 'defensive action'. Trotsky, speaking on behalf of the Soviet, ordered that no troops should be moved out of Petrograd without the authorisation of the MRC.

The MRC and Petrograd's soldiers

The MRC had great authority within Petrograd. Indeed, the city's soldiers and sailors respected the MRC as a true guardian of the revolution. In mid-October Trotsky made sure that the MRC formed close links with all of the units of soldiers in Petrograd.

Write the question

The following sources relate to the role of the Military Revolutionary Committee (MRC) in October 1917. Having read the previous pages about the MRC, write an exam-style question using the sources.

1 How far could the historian make use of Sources 1 and 2 together to investigate … ?

Explain your answer, using both sources, the information given about them and your own knowledge of the historical context.

2 How much weight do you give the evidence of Source 2 for an enquiry into … ?

Explain your answer using the source, the information given about it and your own knowledge of the historical context. **AS**

SOURCE 1

From a report of Trotsky's speech to a conference of representatives of the military garrisons in Petrograd. The conference took place on 21 October. The report appeared in a newspaper edited by Mensheviks and SRs.

After Trotsky's speech, a whole series of people spoke out in regard to the necessity of immediately transferring power to the soviets. Moreover the auditorium became so electrified that when the soldier Goldberg appeared on the stage to say that the transfer of power to the soviets was not wholly clear cut, not only did the assembly break out in shouts of 'Away!' and 'Go to hell!', it completely prevented the speaker from explaining what he had in mind.

The representative of the Fourth Don Cossack Regiment informed the congress that his regiment had decided against participation in the next day's religious procession in order to be ready to defend the revolution.

The representative of the Fourth Don Cossack Regiment caused a sensation when he declared that his regiment would not only refuse to support counter revolutionary moves, they would fight the counter revolution with all their strength. 'In this sense,' said Trotsky, 'I shake hands with my comrade Cossack.' At this Trotsky bent down and shook hands with the Cossack. In response, the assembly exploded in a roar of enthusiastic and thunderous applause, which did not die down for a long time.

SOURCE 2

From Trotsky's Declaration to the Garrisons of Petrograd, written on 21 October.

At a meeting on October 21 the revolutionary garrisons of Petrograd united around the Military Revolutionary Committee, as leader of efforts to halt the counter revolution. Despite this, on the night of October 21 the headquarters of the Petrograd Military Generals refused to recognise the Military Revolutionary Committee. The Generals rejected working in association with the representatives of the Soldiers' Section of the Petrograd Soviet. In so doing the Generals at the headquarters have broken with the revolutionary soldiers and the Petrograd Soviet of Workers' and Soldiers' Deputies.

The Generals at the headquarters have become a direct weapon of counter revolutionary forces.

The protection of revolutionary order from counter revolutionary attacks rests with the revolutionary soldiers directed by the Military Revolutionary Committee. No orders to the garrisons which have not been authorised by the Military Revolutionary Committee should be considered valid.

The revolution is in danger. Long live the revolutionary soldiers!

The events of 24–26 October and the formation of the Bolshevik government

Between 24 and 26 October, Lenin and Trotsky overthrew the Provisional Government.

The fall of the Provisional Government

The first phase of the seizure of power occurred when soldiers loyal to the MRC occupied the post and telegraph offices, as well as the railway stations. In this way, the Bolsheviks extended their control over the city's infrastructure, which prevented the Provisional Government summoning help.

Storming the Winter Palace

The Provisional Government was based in the Winter Palace. The battleship *Aurora* began the assault on the Provisional Government by opening fire on the Winter Palace. Trotsky and the Red Guards successfully arrested the majority of the Provisional Government.

Declaration

On 25 October the MRC announced that the Provisional Government had been 'deposed'. Kerensky fled Petrograd with the support of the American Embassy.

Lenin's new government

The storming of the Winter Palace took place on the day that the Second Congress of Soviets opened. The Bolsheviks did not have a majority of support at the Second Congress of Soviets. Indeed, only 300 of the 670 delegates supported the Bolsheviks.

Creating Sovnarkom

News that Lenin and Trotsky had successfully seized power was greeted by cheers from the Congress. However, some Mensheviks and SRs walked out of the Congress in protest. This reduced Menshevik and SR representation and gave the Bolsheviks a majority at the Congress. Therefore Lenin was able to get support for the creation of a new Bolshevik-dominated government.

The Congress of Soviets voted to create a new constitution. At the top of the new government was the **Sovnarkom** (the Council of People's Commissars). Lenin acted as the chairman of Sovnarkom and was the overall leader of the new government.

Constituent Assembly elections

Following the October Revolution, Lenin claimed that Sovnarkom was the legitimate government of Russia. However, in reality the Bolsheviks had little control of life outside the capital.

Lenin faced a series of obstacles in establishing a new government. Dealing with the elections to the Constituent Assembly was the first major challenge facing the new government.

Lenin refused to cancel the elections. First, the Bolsheviks had criticised the Provisional Government for postponing the elections. Cancelling them would have made the Bolsheviks look like hypocrites. Second, by mid-November Sovnarkom did not have the power to stop the elections taking place.

Election results

The elections were a clear victory for the SRs:

Party	Percentage of vote
SRs	39.5
Bolsheviks	22.5
Kadets	4.5
Mensheviks	3.2

While the Bolsheviks won less than a quarter of the support of the country, the November result marked the high point of Bolshevik support. From December 1917 popular support for Lenin and his party declined.

The consequences of the election

The election results demonstrated that the SRs were clearly Russia's most popular party. However, the Bolsheviks were in a reasonably strong position:
- The SRs were split and therefore weak.
- The Left SRs supported the Sovnarkom; indeed, the first Sovnarkom was a coalition of Left SRs and Bolsheviks. In this sense, Lenin could claim that Sovnarkom was a coalition of Russia's two most popular parties.
- While the elections took place in November the new Assembly was not due to meet until January. This allowed Lenin to postpone conflict between the Bolshevik-dominated Sovnarkom and the new Assembly.

Add the context

Look at the following sample A-level Section A question and the two accompanying sources. Around the edges of the sources, write relevant contextual information that would help you answer the question. Contextual knowledge can include the origin of the source, information about who wrote the source and why.

Tips:

- Don't forget, context also includes the values and beliefs of the society in which the source was written.
- Make sure that the contextual knowledge is relevant to the question set.

How far could the historian make use of Sources 1 and 2 together to investigate the level of popular support for the October Revolution in October 1917?

Explain your answer, using both sources, the information given about them and your own knowledge of the historical context.

SOURCE 1

From a speech made by Boris Kamkov, a leader of the Left Socialist Revolutionaries and a member of the first Sovnarkom. Kamkov was speaking at the First Congress of Left SRs, held in Petrograd in late November 1917.

In late September it became clear that the supporters of revolutionary defencism were unwilling to break with Kerensky's government. Therefore, we looked to the Second Congress of Soviets to take on the task of organising a new government. In our talks with soldiers and workers we emphasised the need for being prepared to provide organised armed support for the Second Congress of Soviets, in case Kerensky's government did not recognise the authority of the newly organised socialist government that they created.

A few days before the Second Congress of Soviets, however, it became clear to those of us working in factories and with the Petrograd garrison, that the Bolsheviks were mobilising their forces not simply to defend the Congress, but rather to seize power in advance of the Congress. In this matter we disagreed drastically with the Bolsheviks. Their plan seemed both dangerous and senseless. After Kerensky's government had so bankrupted itself, after it had become an empty shell, it seemed to us that the Congress could rid us painlessly of the Provisional Government. At the same time, we believed that the Bolshevik plan might appear to be the seizure of power not by the soviets, but by one political party.

SOURCE 2

From the Bolshevik Central Committee, Decision on Armed Uprising, 23 October 1917.

The Central Committee recognises that the international position of the Russian revolution, the military situation, the fact that the Bolshevik party has gained a majority in the Soviets, the peasant revolt and the swing of popular confidence towards our Party in the elections in Moscow, and, finally, the obvious preparations being made for a second Kornilov affair, places an armed uprising on the order of the day.

Considering therefore that an armed uprising is inevitable, and that the time for it is fully ripe, the Central Committee instructs all Party organisations to be guided accordingly. The Party should discuss and decide all practical questions such as the Second Congress of Soviets, the withdrawal of troops from Petrograd, the action of our people in Moscow and other parts of Russia from this point of view.

REVISED

Below is a sample AS Level exam-style question for Section A. Read the model answer and the comments around it.

How much weight do you give the evidence of Source 1 for an enquiry into the development of the 1905 Revolution?

Explain your answer using the source, the information given about it and your own knowledge of the historical context.

SOURCE 1

From Lenin's Lecture on the 1905 Revolution. The lecture was given in Germany in January 1917, while Lenin was in exile. Lenin was speaking to a small group of young radicals.

Prior to January 22 1905, the revolutionary party of Russia consisted of a small group of people. Within a few months, however, the picture changed completely. The hundreds of revolutionary Social-Democrats 'suddenly' grew into thousands; the thousands became the leaders of between two and three million proletarians. The proletarian struggle produced widespread ferment, often revolutionary movements among the peasant masses, fifty to a hundred million strong. The peasant movement had its impact on the army and led to soldiers' revolts, to armed clashes between one section of the army and another. In this manner a colossal country, with a population of 130,000,000, went into the revolution. In this way, dormant Russia was transformed into a Russia of a revolutionary proletariat and a revolutionary people.

The source clearly has some value for an enquiry into the development of the 1905 Revolution. Indeed, Lenin was heavily involved in the revolutionary movement before 1905 and therefore his comments about its growth during the early part of 1905 are useful. However, Lenin does not consider the way in which the revolution was crushed, which clearly limits the value of the source.

The source was written by Lenin in 1917. Lenin was a committed Marxist revolutionary. However, this is no reason to dismiss the source. Indeed, Lenin had joined the Russian Social Democrats in 1893, and by 1905 he was leader of the Bolsheviks, one of the major factions. Therefore, Lenin had an extensive knowledge of underground revolutionary politics before 1905 and therefore his estimates of the size of the movement are likely to be quite reliable. He was also well connected and studied accounts by radicals and the government regarding the growth of the revolution, which may indicate that his estimates for the speed and scale of the growth of the revolutionary movement may be accurate. Indeed, his claim that the armed forces rebelled may be a reference to the Potemkin Mutiny, one of the famous events in the revolution.

However, Lenin's claim that the original revolutionaries 'became the leaders of between two and three million proletarians' is less convincing. From 1902 Lenin argued that Russian workers could not lead a revolution by themselves. Rather he claimed that a 'vanguard party' was necessary to lead the workers. Indeed, this was one of his key differences with the Mensheviks, his rivals within the revolutionary movement. Therefore, this theory may have influenced his perception of the events, or his description of events because his idea of leadership was crucial to his authority within the revolutionary movement and therefore he had a vested interest in describing the revolution in this way.

This is a focused introduction that sets out a range of ways in which the source can be used.

Here the essay uses knowledge of the historical context to evaluate the usefulness of Lenin's comments on the growth of the revolutionary movement.

Lenin's assertion that the revolution had leaders is evaluated in terms of Lenin's values and assumptions.

Finally, the source does not discuss the suppression of the revolution. In this sense it is of little use for understanding the significance of the October Manifesto for the development of the revolution or the military suppression of the Soviets at the end of the year.

In conclusion, the source is partly useful as it is likely to be accurate about the growth of the revolutionary movement during 1905, due to Lenin's knowledge of and connections with the movement. However, Lenin's ideology may well have influenced his description of the role of leaders in the revolution, and finally, the source is clearly limited as it does not consider the Tsar's successful strategy for suppressing the revolution at the end of the year.

The overall value of the source is evaluated in terms of a valid criterion. The conclusion distinguishes between different ways in which the source can be used.

This essay maintains an excellent focus on the question, analysing a variety of ways in which the source can be used. The essay distinguishes between those aspects of the source which reflect Lenin's expert knowledge, those which are based on Lenin's own ideology as well as noting the limitations of the source as a description of the development of the 1905 Revolution. It is therefore a strong answer.

For and against (sources)

It is useful to analyse sample answers such as this by colour coding:
- Evidence that the source is useful
- Evidence that the source is limited.

This helps to analyse how answers can be constructed.

Exam focus (A-level)

Below are an A-level exam-style Section A question and a sample answer. Read the answer and the comments around it.

Study Sources 1 and 2. How far could the historian make use of Sources 1 and 2 together to investigate conflicting attitudes to the continuation of the war during 1917?

Explain your answer, using both sources, the information given about them and your own knowledge of the historical context.

SOURCE 1

From an article by Joseph Stalin published in *Pravda*, on 26 March 1917.

In the interview he gave on March 23, Mr Milyukov, Minister of Foreign Affairs, outlined his 'programme' on the aims of the present war. Our readers will know from yesterday's *Pravda* that these aims are imperialistic: seizure of Constantinople, seizure of Armenia, partition of Austria and Turkey, seizure of Northern Persia.

It appears that the Russian soldiers are shedding their blood on the battlefields not in 'defence of the fatherland,' and not 'for freedom,' as the venal bourgeois press assures us, but for the seizure of foreign territories in the interests of a handful of imperialists.

That, at least, is what Mr Milyukov says.

In whose name does Mr Milyukov say all this so frankly and so publicly?

Not, of course, in the name of the Russian people. Because the Russian people – the Russian workers, peasants and soldiers – are opposed to the seizure of foreign territories, opposed to the violation of nations. This is eloquently attested by the 'appeal' of the Petrograd Soviet of Workers' and Soldiers' Deputies, the spokesman of the will of the Russian people.

If Kerensky is to be believed, Mr Milyukov does not express the opinion of the Provisional Government on the central question of the war aims.

SOURCE 2

From an appeal issued by the Provisional Government on 20 June 1917.

Citizens. The army of free Russia has started the offensive.

By defending liberty and the independence of the fatherland they are selflessly fulfilling their duty to the country.

In this awe-inspiring historic hour when the fate of Russia depends on the combat might of the army, on the might and the enthusiasm of all the country, the Provisional Government appeals to you, to give all your will, all your strength in a common effort with the army, to save the revolution and the fatherland from mortal danger.

In the face of great sufferings, the Provisional Government calls you to realise your exceptional responsibility, and to renounce everything that leads to disunity, dedicating all your forces to the defence of liberty and of Russia.

Let the army of Revolutionary Russia know that while going to defend the revolution, while going to die for the eternal ideals of freedom, it had behind it the whole people of Russia which, like itself, is ready to perform this heroic task.

Sources 1 and 2 are useful for an investigation into the conflicting attitudes to the continuation of the war during 1917 as they contain clear statements of the two main views at the time. Additionally, the two sources were written at crucial moments in 1917. In that sense they give a picture of the development of the debate. In this context the sources are useful because they imply there was a growing desire for peace during 1917.

The essay starts by setting out a range of ways in which the sources might be useful for the enquiry the question focuses on.

Sources 1 and 2 are valuable as they contain important views on the continuation of the War. Stalin's argument, in Source 1, that Milyukov wanted to continue the war in order to conquer territory, is wholly plausible. Stalin was writing in late March, at a time when Milyukov was Minister of Foreign Affairs, and his ally Guchkov was Minister for War. These two liberals supported the overthrow of the Tsar in order to ensure that the government could fight the war more effectively. Moreover, in mid-April Milyukov's telegram explicitly set out his desire to achieve a victory in order to seize territory. While Stalin's description of this position as being motivated by the 'interests of a handful of imperialists' is clearly political, his fundamental description of Milyukov's aims is plausible in the context.

Source 1 and Source 2 also set out an alternative view: 'revolutionary defencism'. Source 1 states that Kerensky disagreed with Milyukov's view. Source 2 was published in June 1917, at a time when Kerensky was Minister for War and preparing the June Offensive. Therefore, it is likely to reflect his view. Source 2 justifies the war to 'save the revolution and the fatherland from mortal danger'. Source 2 was written at a time when Menshevik Tsereteli was part of the government. He was the first advocate of 'revolutionary defencism'. Again this indicates that Source 2 advocates that position.

Finally, Sources 1 and 2 indicate that by June 'revolutionary defencism' was less popular than it had been. Source 2 urges Russians to 'renounce everything that leads to disunity'. Indeed, it was written in June after the Milyukov crisis had undermined confidence in the Provisional Government's reasons for continuing the war. Therefore, Source 2 is useful because it implies that the Bolshevik position of seeking a 'democratic peace' was gaining ground. Source 1 also indicates this. Stalin was committed to ending the war throughout 1917. Nonetheless, his article in March doesn't say that. Rather he attacks Milyukov by implying that a battle in 'defence of the fatherland' and for 'freedom' was a better policy. Indeed, Stalin praised the Appeal of the Petrograd Soviet which, as the source shows, supported 'revolutionary defencism'. Stalin's refusal to call explicitly for peace may well have been motivated by his desire to appeal to the mainstream of the revolutionary movement, which in March, supported 'revolutionary defencism'.

Overall, Sources 1 and 2 are useful because they set out two of the three main positions. They also imply that the Bolshevik view gained ground from March to June. Sources 1 and 2 are much less useful for investigating attitudes to the continuation of the war after June; a historian would need other sources to understand what happened to the debate from June to December.

This paragraph explains the way in which Sources 1 and 2 relate to the debate about the war going on in Russia at the time. In this way it discusses the sources in the context of their time.

Here the essay integrates detailed contextual knowledge to evaluate the reliability of Stalin's claims about Milyukov's policy towards the war.

This paragraph makes intelligent inferences, based on the sources and contextual knowledge about the changing appeal of revolutionary defencism.

This paragraph summarises the argument of the essay and also discusses a prime limitation of the sources.

This is another strong essay. It interrogates the evidence of both sources with confidence. This is clear from the inferences it makes about the implications of Sources 1 and 2. It uses knowledge of the historical context to weigh the evidence of the sources and reach a judgement about the reliability of different aspects of the sources. The conclusion also discusses an important limitation of the sources. However, the essay could have been improved by bringing this into the essay earlier.

For and against (sources)

It is useful to analyse sample answers such as this by colour coding:
- Evidence that the source is useful
- Evidence that the source is limited.

This helps to analyse how answers can be constructed.

4 Defending the Bolshevik revolution, October 1917–24

Consolidating Bolshevik power

Lenin's new government faced a series of problems which threatened to end Bolshevik rule:
- Continuing war with Germany.
- Limited support in the countryside.
- Major food shortages in the cities.
- A large proportion of Russian workers were on strike.

The threat of the Constituent Assembly

One of Lenin's most pressing problems was the Constituent Assembly. Lenin knew that the Socialist Revolutionaries (SRs) had won the largest number of seats in the November elections. This created problems for Lenin as the SRs would use the election result to try to establish a rival government.

Closing the Assembly

The Constituent Assembly met on 5 January 1918 and rejected Lenin's demand that the Constituent Assembly should be subservient to the Sovnarkom. In response, Lenin ordered the Red Guards to close the Assembly after a single day.

The impact of the closure

Most Russians had hoped that the Constituent Assembly would begin to rebuild Russia. Therefore, while many radical workers supported the closure, Lenin's action was unpopular with the majority of Russians.

Workers' response

Many workers accepted the closure of the Constituent Assembly. They believed that the new government genuinely represented their interests because Sovnarkom:
- issued the Decree on Workers' Control, which gave workers the right to control all aspects of production
- decreed a maximum eight-hour day.

Making peace at Brest-Litovsk

Lenin was determined to end the First World War. He knew that the war had been one of the key reasons for the collapse of the Tsar's regime and the Provisional Government.
- He believed that ending the war was essential to the survival of the new government. He hoped that ending the war would give the economy a chance to recover, which would create a 'breathing space' for the new government.
- Lenin believed that a civil war was inevitable. Ending Russia's involvement in the First World War would allow his government to recall troops, ready to fight the Bolsheviks' opponents when civil war broke out.

Peace negotiations

Lenin appointed Trotsky to conduct the peace negotiations with the Germans in the town of Brest-Litovsk. The German demands were very harsh. They demanded:
- the Baltic states, which included Latvia, Lithuania and Estonia
- Poland
- the Ukraine, an important agricultural region.

The above meant that Russia would lose:
- 32 per cent of its arable land
- 26 per cent of its railway system
- 33 per cent of its factories
- 75 per cent of its coal and iron ore mines.

Divisions over the peace deal

Many Bolsheviks opposed the peace agreement:
- Bukharin advocated fighting a revolutionary war against capitalist and imperialist nations to spread the revolution across Europe.
- Trotsky advocated a policy of 'neither peace nor war'. He argued that the truce should continue without a formal peace treaty.

Lenin forces peace

Lenin threatened to resign from the government unless senior Bolsheviks backed the policy. This threat forced Lenin's opponents to back down. On 3 March 1918, Trotsky signed the Treaty of Brest-Litovsk.

The consequence of peace

The closure of the Constituent Assembly had been controversial. However, ending the war created an even greater crisis. Together these two actions turned public opinion away from the new government.

Break with the Left SRs

The treaty was extremely unpopular as it resulted in massive losses of land. The Left SRs, who had supported the government and participated in the Sovnarkom, resigned from government in protest at the treaty.

Explain the difference

The following sources give different accounts of the problems facing the Tsarist system during the First World War. List the ways in which the sources differ. Explain the differences between the sources using the provenance of the sources, and the historical context. The provenance appears at the top of the source. Make sure you stay focused on the differences that are relevant to the question.

How far could the historian make use of Sources 1 and 2 together to investigate popular reactions to the closure of the Constituent Assembly in January 1918?

Explain your answer, using both sources, the information given about them and your own knowledge of the historical context.

The two sources appear to disagree on the popular reactions to the closure of the Constituent Assembly in January 1918 because ...

_____

_____

Tip: remember to refer to the specific context of the time when analysing the sources.

SOURCE 1

From a declaration by the Petrograd Union to Defend the Constituent Assembly, published on 6 January 1918. The Declaration was published as part of a protest march which took place on 6 January in support of the Constituent Assembly. The union was created in November 1917 by Kadets, Mensheviks and some Right SRs.

The Petrograd Union to Defend the Constituent Assembly has called on all the population of the city of Petrograd to take part in a demonstration in honour of the opening of the Constituent Assembly.

The demonstration is to be peaceful and to be held under the following slogan: 'All Power to the Constituent Assembly' and 'Down with the Civil War.'

The Sovnarkom has called out two thousand sailors to guard the Tauride Palace* and the streets surrounding it.

The Petrograd Soviet has passed a resolution that asks honest workers and soldiers not to oppose the Constituent Assembly. Workers should remain in their factories and soldiers in the barracks.

At about 11:30 the demonstration started. About two hundred men bearing a flag with the words 'All Power to the Constituent Assembly', approached the Tauride Palace. Armed soldiers and Red Guards appeared and demanded that the crowd disperse. When the crowd continued marching they fired. The crowd ran.

* Tauride Palace: the meeting place of the Constituent Assembly

SOURCE 2

From the Decree of the Central Executive Committee of the Petrograd Soviet dissolving the Constituent Assembly, issued on 8 January 1918.

From the beginning of the Russian Revolution the Soviets brought the exploited masses together and led them in the fight for full political and economic freedom. The Soviets learned by experience that it was pointless to compromise with the bourgeoisie. They learned about the deception of bourgeois-democracy. The Soviets came to the conclusion that it is not possible to free working people without rejecting compromises with the bourgeoisie. The October Revolution was the final break with the bourgeoisie.

The Constituent Assembly was elected on the basis of lists made before the October Revolution. It represents compromise with the Cadets and bourgeois power.

Working people have learned by experience that bourgeois parliaments, like the Constituent Assembly, have outlived their usefulness. To deny full power to the Soviets in favour of the Constituent Assembly would be a step backward and a death blow to the October Revolution.

In view of this, the Central Executive Committee of the Petrograd Soviet hereby decrees: the Constituent Assembly is dissolved.

The Cheka and the Red Terror

Sovnarkom established the **Cheka**, the new regime's political police, in December 1917. The Cheka, or Extraordinary Commission for Combating Counter-Revolution and Sabotage, embodied Lenin's views on revolutionary violence. Lenin believed that in times of emergency revolutionaries needed to defend their government with force.

The role of the Cheka

The Cheka targeted the right, then the left:
- Initially, the Cheka closed right-wing papers. Indeed, in November 1917 the Kadets were outlawed.
- In December 1917 Lenin authorised the arrest of leading members of the Right SRs and right-wing Mensheviks such as Tsereteli.
- In April 1918 the Bolsheviks expelled the SRs and the Mensheviks from the Soviets, claiming that they were **counter-revolutionaries**.

The Cheka did not enforce laws. Nor were they bound by laws. Rather they dispensed 'revolutionary justice', which allowed them to act arbitrarily.

The Mensheviks and SRs remained legal until 1922. However, attacks by the Cheka meant that the parties disintegrated. Some Mensheviks and SRs joined the Bolshevik Party. Others, around 2 million, fled Russia, or ended up in the Cheka's labour camps.

The Cheka's methods

The Cheka were authorised by Sovnarkom to shoot suspects without trial and to use torture. The Cheka's victims were sometimes:
- scalped
- allowed to freeze and turned into frozen statues
- skinned
- mutilated
- eaten by starving rats
- branded
- crucified (in the case of priests).

These forms of torture were designed, in part, to terrify Russians into obeying the new government.

Felix Dzerzhinsky

Felix Dzerzhinsky was the first head of the Cheka. His headquarters were in the Lubyanka in Moscow. Dzerzhinsky was ideologically committed to the use of terror against counter-revolutionaries, and was an advocate of swift and harsh revolutionary justice. He was known as 'Iron Felix' due to his ruthlessness.

The Cheka and the Civil War, 1918–21

During the Civil War, the Cheka's role was to protect Communist rule in areas held by the Communists. The Red Army, by contrast, were responsible for defending and enlarging Communist-held territory.

From 1918 to 1921 the Cheka used terror in a variety of ways. The Cheka:
- helped the Red Army requisition grain from the peasants as part of **War Communism** (see page 70)
- closed down opposition newspapers and imprisoned, tortured and executed socialist opponents of the new government
- used extreme violence against the enemies of the Communist Party in recently captured areas; violence was often public in order to terrify the population of recently captured areas into submission
- supported the Red Army's attack on the Kronstadt naval base; Cheka agents with machine guns were positioned behind Red Army soldiers and instructed to shoot any soldiers who retreated or refused to fight
- ran concentration camps that housed the Communists' enemies
- stopped private trading, which was outlawed under War Communism.

Red Terror

The Cheka unleashed a wave of 'Red Terror' at the end of August 1918. This was a response to a failed assassination attempt on Lenin.

The scale of the terror

In September around 15,000 people were executed by the Cheka. Estimates of the number killed by the Cheka between 1918 and 1921 vary from 50,000 to 3 million.

The impact of the terror

As support for the Bolsheviks diminished, the new government relied increasingly on fear. Dzerzhinsky boasted that the actions of the Cheka underpinned all of the achievements of Lenin's government.

The Cheka transformed Russian politics, effectively ending:
- press freedom
- freedom of speech
- opposition groups.

Identify an argument

Below are a series of definitions, a sample exam question and two sample conclusions. One of the conclusions achieves a high mark because it contains an argument. The other achieves a lower mark because it contains only description and assertion. Identify which is which. The mark scheme on page 90 will help you.

Description: a detailed account.

Assertion: a statement of fact or an opinion which is not supported by a reason.

Reason: a statement which explains or justifies something.

Argument: an assertion justified with a reason.

> How significant was the role of the Red Terror in the development of Lenin's government in the years 1917–21?

In conclusion, the Red Terror was one factor that significantly affected the development of Lenin's government in the years 1917–21. The Terror led to the consolidation of the regime. Equally, economic problems influenced the development of the regime as they led to changes in economic policy. Finally, specific decisions affected the development of the regime, such as the decision to sign a peace treaty with Germany. This resulted in growing opposition to the regime. Therefore, the Red Terror was one of several factors that significantly affected the development of Lenin's government in the years 1917–21.

Overall, the Red Terror was the most significant factor in the development of Lenin's government in the years 1917–21. This is because the Red Terror changed the nature of government. In 1917 Lenin governed as the dominant partner in a coalition. What is more, other political parties played a role in the Soviets across Russia, and freely published newspapers and organised political opposition to the government. The Red Terror changed this. Government became dominated by the Bolsheviks, the Soviets ceased to make political decisions, opposition parties were persecuted, and freedom of expression was destroyed. In that sense, while there were other important influences on the development of government, the Red Terror was the most significant factor because it changed the nature of Russian government from democracy to dictatorship.

Identify the criteria

Read the question and the two sample conclusions again. One of them uses clear criteria to make a judgement. Summarise the criteria below:

Criteria:

_____

_____

Now summarise why these criteria help answer the question and support a judgement:

_____

_____

Bolshevik economic policies

Lenin's economic policy changed radically over time. Policy changes reflected Lenin's changing objectives:

- In the short term, Lenin wanted to stabilise the economy and generate economic growth. He hoped this would win popularity for the new regime.
- From mid-1918 Lenin's key objective was to win the Civil War.
- After 1921 he needed to rebuild and stabilise the regime.

The evolution of Lenin's policies also reflected **Marxist ideology**. Marx was clear that a Communist society would have an extremely advanced economy. Therefore Lenin was committed to the modernisation of the Russian economy.

State capitalism

In essence, state capitalism was based on the nationalisation of industry. Nationalisation ended capitalism by passing the ownership of industry from capitalists to the new state.

Lenin hoped that nationalisation would lead to greater efficiency as the government could employ experts to run the economy. Control of the nationalised industries was then centralised by the **Vesenkha** which would:

- re-establish worker discipline by offering higher pay to productive workers
- ensure factories were properly managed by placing them under the control of well-paid specialists
- co-ordinate economic production to meet the needs of the new society.

The consequences of state capitalism

State capitalism was extremely unpopular as it ended workers' control. Moreover, the government kept wages low, as Lenin wanted to target resources at economic growth. Finally, the Vesenkha tended to employ former factory owners to manage the state-controlled factories. In this sense, life for the workers in factories under state capitalism was very similar to life before the Revolution.

War Communism

From mid-1918 Lenin introduced a series of emergency economic measures. Together these became known as War Communism, a series of policies designed to ensure Communist victory in the Civil War.

Food dictatorship

War Communism abolished the free market in food by introducing a food dictatorship. The food dictatorship consisted of:

- grain requisitioning – Cheka squads were authorised to seize grain and other forms of food from peasants without payment
- rationing – the Supply Commissariat rationed the seized foods. The largest rations went to workers and soldiers, the smallest rations were given to members of the bourgeoisie.

Labour discipline

War Communism also entailed intense labour discipline:

- In 1918 the working day was extended to 11 hours.
- In 1919 work was made compulsory for all able-bodied people between 16 and 50 years of age.
- Harsh punishments were given to workers who were late or caught slacking.

The abolition of the market

The chaotic conditions of the Civil War led to a breakdown of the existing market. Bukharin and other radicals saw this a huge victory; they believed that the Revolution had destroyed the capitalist market. The following measures were introduced to try to abolish the market:

- The abolition of money. In the short term, the government simply printed more money, which led to **hyperinflation**. Money became worthless, workers were paid through their rations, and many public services, such as trams, were provided freely.
- The abolition of trade. Private trade was made illegal.
- Complete nationalisation. All businesses were taken over by the state.

The consequences of War Communism

War Communism destroyed incentives to work. Consequently, there was an economic catastrophe. By 1920 there was a famine in the countryside. Additionally, workers fled the cities in search of food. In total, the industrial workforce declined from 2.6 million workers in 1917 to 1.2 million in early 1921.

Spot the inference

High-level answers avoid excessive summarising or paraphrasing the sources. Instead they make inferences from the sources, as well as analysing their value in terms of their context. Below is a source and a series of statements. Read the source and decide which of the statements:

- infer from the source (I)
- paraphrase the source (P)
- summarise the source (S)
- cannot be justified from the source (X).

Fill in the boxes below with either I, P, S or X:

- The Constituent Assembly was elected by the Russian people. ☐
- The writers of Source 1 believe that Sovnarkom is pursuing counter revolutionary policies. ☐
- The writers of Source 1 do not believe that all Bolsheviks are counter-revolutionaries. ☐
- The Left SRs believe that the Treaty of Brest-Litovsk was forced on Russia by the Germans. ☐
- The writers of Source 1 believe the Left SRs should start a terrorist campaign against Sovnarkom, to save the values of the Russian Revolution. ☐
- The writers of Source 1 believe that terrorist action will inspire the workers and peasants to rise up against the government. ☐
- The Left SRs want to assassinate Lenin. ☐

SOURCE 1

A resolution passed by the Central Committee of the Left SRs. The resolution was passed in Moscow on 24 June 1918.

The Central Committee of the Left SR Party, having examined the present political situation, resolves that in the interests of the Russian revolution, an immediate end must be put to the so-called 'breathing space' created by the Treaty of Brest Litovsk. The Central Committee believes it to be possible and practical to organise a series of terrorist acts against the leaders of the Bolshevik government. At the same time – in order to carry out its decisions – the Central Committee of the Left SR Party resolves to mobilise all reliable armed forces and take extreme measures to make the peasants and workers take part in the uprising against the government.

All local branches of the Left SR Party must prepare to take vigorous action against the present policy of Sovnarkom. Acts of terrorism should start after a signal from the Left SR Party in Moscow.

We regard our policy as an attack on Sovnarkom, not as an attack on the Bolsheviks themselves. However, as the Bolsheviks may take aggressive counter action against our Party, we are determined, if necessary, to defend ourselves with the force of arms.

The crisis of 1921

By early 1921, the Communists had won the Civil War. However, the Civil War had created a political and economic crisis.

The Tambov rising

From the autumn of 1920, peasants in Tambov, led by Aleksandr Antonov, began a rebellion against Communist grain requisitioning and Cheka brutality. By January 1921 Antonov had a force of 50,000 anti-Communist fighters. Antonov's revolt spread throughout the spring of 1921.

The Kronstadt Mutiny

In early 1921 there was a wave of strikes across Russia's main cities. In Petrograd the Red Army responded by opening fire on unarmed workers.

Sailors at the Kronstadt naval base rebelled against Communist brutality. The mutineers demanded a series of reforms, including:

- an immediate free and fair election of new Soviets
- release of all anarchist, Menshevik and SR political prisoners
- a restoration of freedom of speech and the press
- the abolition of the Cheka
- an end to War Communism (see page 70)
- ending of the political domination of the Communists.

Lenin's response

The scale of the Tambov rebellion and Kronstadt Mutiny frightened senior Communists. Lenin responded swiftly:

- In mid-March the Red Army had crushed the Kronstadt uprising. Mikhail Tukhachevski, a former White General (see page 74), attacked the naval base with 60,000 troops, backed by several thousand armed members of the Cheka. Over 3,000 of the mutineers were killed or injured.
- Tukhachevski was also dispatched to Tambov to end the rebellion. In May he suppressed the rebellion by deporting 100,000 people to labour camps and attacking peasant villages with poison gas.

The New Economic Policy

Lenin's ruthlessness showed that there would be no political compromise. Nonetheless, Lenin was willing to embrace economic change. Indeed, as a result of the unrest he introduced the New Economic Policy (NEP).

Measures

The NEP ended War Communism by creating a **mixed economy**:

- Farming was left to the free market. Peasants could buy, sell and produce freely. Grain requisitioning ended and was replaced by a **tax in kind**.
- Small factories and workshops were denationalised and allowed to trade freely. Many were returned to their former capitalist owners.
- Large factories and major industries remained nationalised.
- Money was reintroduced.

The consequences of the NEP

The NEP led to political and economic stability. However, it did not lead to rapid industrial growth. Nor was it wholly popular within the party.

Farming

Ending grain requisitioning was extremely popular among the peasants. Free trade also encouraged peasants to grow more food. Therefore the famine ended and farming revived.

Industry

The NEP also led to industrial growth. Lenin authorised a major electrification campaign which revived an industry that had effectively been destroyed by the Civil War. However, industrial recovery was extremely slow.

The ban on factions

Lenin coupled economic reform with much tighter political control. At the same time as introducing the NEP, Lenin introduced a ban on factions within the Communist Party. Members of the Communist Party were not allowed to form groups that were independent from Lenin's control. Lenin also supported 'democratic centralism', which meant all other political parties were banned and decisions made by Lenin and the **Politburo** had to be supported by all Communists.

Add the context

Look at the following sample A-level Section A question and the two accompanying sources. Around the edges of the sources, write relevant contextual information that would help you answer the question. Contextual knowledge can include the origin of the source, information about who wrote the source and why.

Tips:

● Don't forget, context also includes the values and beliefs of the society in which the source was written.

● Make sure that the contextual knowledge is relevant to the question set.

How far could the historian make use of Sources 1 and 2 together to investigate the problems Lenin's government in 1920–21? Explain your answer, using both sources, the information given about them and your own knowledge of the historical context.

SOURCE 1

From the Resolution passed at the General Meeting of the Kronstadt sailors held on 1 March 1921.

Having heard the report of the crew representatives, sent to the City of Petrograd by the General Meeting of ships' crews for clarification of the situation there, we resolve:

1. In view of the fact that the present Soviets do not express the will of the workers and peasants, we resolve to immediately hold new elections to the Soviets by secret ballot, with freedom of pre-election agitation for all workers and peasants.

2. Freedom of speech and press for workers and peasants, anarchists and socialist parties.

3. Freedom of assembly of both trades unions and peasant associations.

4. To convene not later than March 10th, 1921 a Conference of workers, soldiers and sailors of the city of Petrograd, of Kronstadt, and of Petrograd province.

5. To free all political prisoners of socialist parties, and also all workers and peasants, soldiers and sailors imprisoned in connection with worker and peasant movements.

...

10. To abolish the Communist fighting detachments in all military units, and also the various guards kept in factories and plants by the Communists, and if such guards or detachments are needed, they can be chosen in military units from the companies, and in factories and plants by the discretion of the workers.

11. To give the peasants full control over their own land, to do as they wish, and also to keep cattle, which must be maintained and managed by their own strength, that is, without using hired labour.

SOURCE 2

From a report by Aleksandr Shlikhter, an expert on food supplies. Shlikhter worked in Michurinsk, a town in the Tambov region. Shlikhter sent the report to Lenin and the leaders of the Communist Military.

1. The rebellion has overtaken the three most grain-rich regions of the province: Tambov, Kirsanov and Borisoglebsk.

2. The forces currently available to suppress the rebellion are 3,500 men. Included in that number are: units of Tambov military cadets, grain procurement squads and Cheka units sent as reinforcement from neighbouring regions.

3. The Tambov Military Council considers it possible to suppress the rebellion, but only under the following conditions:
   a) The liquidation of the rebellion will require no fewer than 4 weeks.
   b) Surrounding and destroying the bandits, including those who have appeared in the south, is not possible with the troops now available.

4. Procurement work has for the time being been halted. Continuation of the rebellion will result in the abandonment of all procurement work.

5. Fulfilment of the procurement targets can only be guaranteed after the liquidation of the rebellion.

Civil War

The rebellion of the **Czech Legions** on 25 May 1918 signalled the start of the Civil War. During the summer of 1918, anti-Communist armies were established in Siberia, Estonia and in the Ukraine.

The Civil War raged from mid-1918 to early 1921, ending in Communist victory.

Reds, Whites and Greens

There were a number of different groups fighting during the Russian Civil War.
- The **Reds**: Communist forces.
- The **Whites**: liberals, Tsarists or those who wanted to establish a military dictatorship.
- The '**Greens**': associated with the Left SRs or anarchist groups. They fought for the **autonomy** of local groups of peasants.
- Nationalists also fought to free their homelands from Russian domination.

The geography of the Civil War

The Reds had a strong geographical position which helped them win the Civil War.

Red strengths	Opposition weaknesses
The Reds controlled: - the most densely populated areas, containing around 70 million people, and were therefore able to recruit workers and soldiers - Russia's most industrialised regions, which meant they could produce the weapons and equipment necessary to win victory - the land containing Russia's main rail lines, which meant that they were able to transport goods and equipment to support their army throughout the Civil War.	The Whites controlled: - fewer people, only around 20 million, and therefore they had fewer workers and soldiers - few factories, and therefore they did not have the capacity to produce munitions - regions in the far north, east and south. Therefore, their forces were divided and difficult to co-ordinate. General Yudenich was based in Estonia, General Denikin in southern Russia and Admiral Kolchak was based in the north.

The Green position

Nestor Makhno's Green forces controlled a small area of the Ukraine. Therefore, their resources were limited, both in terms of their population and ability to produce weapons.

Trotsky and the Red Army

In March 1918 Lenin reformed the army:
- Democratic control was abolished.
- Trotsky, the leader of the new army, put Tsarist generals back in charge of the army.
- Each battalion was placed under dual command. Former Tsarist generals were forced to work with political commissars in order to command the new army. Political commissars were introduced in order to ensure that the old generals, who were often still loyal to the Tsar, did not sabotage the new army.

These reforms outraged **idealists** in the party, who accused Lenin and Trotsky of betraying the principles of the revolution. Nonetheless, they turned the Red Army into a disciplined and successful fighting force.

Trotsky's role

Trotsky played an important role in Red victory:
- Trotsky was loyal to Lenin; the two agreed on the fundamental principles of winning the war.
- Trotsky was a very effective leader of the Red Army. This could be seen when he sent reinforcements to Petrograd and prevented General Yudenich from seizing control of Petrograd.
- Trotsky used an armoured train to visit and support areas under threat.
- Trotsky deployed skilful tactics. For example, he formed an alliance with Nestor Makhno's Green Revolutionary Insurgent Army of the Ukraine in order to beat White forces in the Ukraine. However, once the Whites were defeated the Reds turned on their former allies.

RAG – rate the timeline

Look at the following sample exam question and timeline. Read the question, study the timeline and, using three coloured pens, put a Red, Amber or Green star next to the events to show:

Red: events and policies that have no relevance to the question

Amber: events and policies that have some significance to the question

Green: events and policies that are directly relevant to the question

'The survival and consolidation of Communist government in Russia, in the years 1918–21, owed more to Trotsky's leadership of the Red Army than to the weaknesses of the opposition.' How far do you agree with this statement?

Now repeat the activity with the following questions:

How significant was Lenin's role in the development of the Communist regime in the years to his death?

How far did Lenin's policies change in the period 1918–21? **AS**

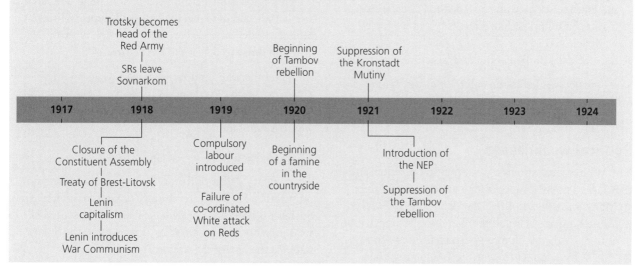

Spectrum of importance

Below is a sample exam question and a list of general points which could be used to answer the question. Use your own knowledge and the information on the opposite page to reach a judgement about the importance of these general points to the question posed. Write their numbers on the spectrum below to indicate their relative importance.

'The weaknesses and divisions of the opposition were primarily responsible for Communist victory in the Civil War (1918–21).' How far do you agree with this statement?

1 Weaknesses and divisions of the opposition

2 War Communism

3 Trotsky's leadership of the Red Army

4 Support for the Communists

← Less important   Very important →

Having done this, write a brief justification of your placement, explaining why some of these factors are more important than others. The resulting diagram could form the basis of an essay plan.

Defeat of domestic enemies

The Communists triumphed over their domestic enemies for a variety of reasons.

The defeat of Kolchak, Denikin and Yudenich

The Whites were weak because of their strategic position. They were spread out over a large area:

- Admiral Alexander Kolchak led reactionary forces in Siberia.
- General Nikolai Yudenich led White forces in the north-east.
- General Anton Denikin and Petr Wrangel's forces were based in the south.

Therefore:

- they often failed to co-ordinate attacks – for example, General Deniken's forces were concentrated in the south-east of Russia; he failed to co-ordinate his attacks with Kolchak effectively and his forces were defeated
- they lacked a unified command structure and strategy.

These difficulties led to the failure of major White military initiatives, such as a united attack on the Reds in March 1919.

Political weaknesses

The Whites were also in a weak political position. Indeed they lacked popular support for a variety of reasons:

- Many Russians identified the Whites with Tsarism.
- Some Russians believed the Whites were unpatriotic as they worked with foreign invaders (see page 78).
- The Whites fought to keep the Empire together. However, they were based outside Russia's heartland. Therefore they did not have the support of the local non-Russian populations, who wanted independence from the Russian Empire.
- Leading White generals fought to end democracy, which was unpopular with most workers and peasants. Indeed, moderate socialists supported the Reds at some points in the war in order to stop the Whites establishing a dictatorship.
- Leading Whites promised to take land away from the peasants, which was unpopular with the majority of the Russian population.

The death of the Tsar

The execution of Tsar Nicholas II in July 1918 weakened the Whites. His death meant that the Whites no longer had a figurehead to unite around. Equally, the execution of the royal family clearly ended the possibility of restoring Tsarism.

Defeating the Social Revolutionaries

Having won the election to the Constituent Assembly, the SRs attempted to set up their own government in Samara, an area that was outside Communist control in 1918.

SR defeat

Komuch, the SR government, had the support of the Czech Legion which comprised 50,000 men. The SRs also had the aid of General Vladimir Kappel, a Tsarist military leader who was prepared to work with any group in order to defeat the Red Army.

In September the Red Army began to attack. The SRs were unable to defend themselves, and therefore Komuch and SR attempts to create a democratic socialist republic failed.

Show trials

The military defeat of Komuch did not end Lenin's war on the SRs. In 1922 Dzerzhinsky organised the trial of Socialist Revolutionary leaders. They were accused of treason, sabotage and plotting to overthrow the Soviet state. At the end of the trial in August 1922 all of the defendants were sentenced to death. Most were, however, imprisoned and executed a decade later.

Defeating National minorities

Immediately after the October Revolution, Lenin published the Declaration of the Rights of the Peoples of Russia, guaranteeing all of national minorities in the former Russian Empire the right to self-determination.

However, Lenin's government did not fulfil these promises. Latvia, Estonia and Lithuania gained independence from Russia with German help. Poland defeated the Communists in war, and in so doing won its freedom. The government of the Georgian Mensheviks, however, was defeated by the Red Army in 1921.

(i) You're the examiner

Below are a sample exam question and a paragraph written in answer to this question. Read the paragraph and the mark scheme provided on page 90. Decide which level you would award the paragraph and write a justification for your choice.

How significant were the weaknesses of the Communists' opponents in bringing about Communist victory in the Russian Civil War?

The weaknesses of the Communists' opponents were significant in bringing about Communist victory to an extent. The Whites were divided, as they had different leaders in different parts of Russia, like Wrangel. Also the Whites were not popular, as many Russians associated them with the Tsar. Peasants feared that the Whites would take away their land. Also the SRs and the Whites disagreed on ideology so they could not unite against the Reds.

(i) Turning assertion into argument

Below are a sample exam question and a series of assertions. Read the exam question and then add a justification to each of the assertions to turn it into an argument.

How far did divisions among the Communists' opponents lead to Communist victory in the Civil War (1918–21)?

Divisions among the Communists' opponents led to Communist victory in the Civil War because ...

_____

_____

War Communism also helped the Communists win the Civil War because ...

_____

_____

Trotsky's leadership of the Red Army was another reason for Communist victory because ...

_____

_____

The Whites did not have much popular support, which helped the Reds win the Civil War because ...

_____

_____

Foreign intervention in Russia

In addition to fighting the Whites and the Greens, the new government was forced to fight a range of foreign enemies – capitalist countries such as the US, France and Britain.

The reasons for intervention

The countries involved attacked Russia for a variety of reasons. Russia's former allies invaded in order to:

- try to change the government, hoping that a new government would re-enter the war
- ensure that the munitions that they had sent to Russia were not captured by the Germans.

Additionally, France invaded in order to put pressure on the Russian government to pay back its debts. The British also invaded for ideological reasons. Winston Churchill, who was in the British cabinet at the time, wanted to stop the spread of **Communism**.

The Japanese government, recognising Russia's weakness, occupied parts of Siberia in order to extend the Japanese Empire.

The nature of foreign intervention

Britain, France, Japan and the US all sent troops to Russia.

- Allied troops occupied strategic ports including Murmansk in the Arctic, Archangel on the White Sea and Odessa on the Black Sea.
- In 1918, British troops occupied part of central Asia.
- In April 1918, Japanese troops captured the port of Vladivostok.

In 1918 there were around 200,000 foreign troops in Russia. However, Allied troops tended to play a defensive role. They defended supply depots and ports from Red attacks, but they rarely engaged in attacks on Red territory.

Economic intervention

The Whites benefited from foreign economic aid:

- The British sent around £100 millions' worth of supplies to the Whites.
- The French agreed to give loans of money and equipment to Wrangel on condition that the Whites would pay back existing French loans if they won the Civil War.

- The US gave more than $50 million of interest-free loans, and the US president authorised shipments of over 250,000 rifles, clothing and food to aid the Whites. The US sent approximately $77 millions' worth of aid to the Whites in 1919.

The impact of war weariness

Western intervention was hampered by the war weariness of the public and the soldiers. At the end of the First World War there was little British, American or French support for another, potentially lengthy military campaign.

Allied troops were also unwilling to fight in Russia. First, many working-class troops had some sympathy with the goals of the Communists. They certainly could see no reason to support landowners, and Tsarists.

Impact on the Communists

Allied intervention did not present major military problems for Lenin's new government. The vast majority of British, French and US troops withdrew in mid to late 1919. Once the First World War was over Allied governments stopped sending aid to the Whites. With the war over there was no incentive for the western powers to install a new government that was willing to fight Germany.

Propaganda victory

The Communists were able to turn foreign intervention to their advantage. Communist propaganda portrayed foreign intervention as an attack on the Russian motherland. They were also able to argue that the Whites were unpatriotic as they were allied to Russia's foreign enemies.

Lenin's legacy

Lenin died in January 1924. Having promised peace, land and bread, he had led Russia into a brutal civil war and his policies had created a famine. Soviet democracy had been usurped by the party. Nonetheless, Lenin had succeeded in his prime goal: the Communists had seized and retained power. Lenin hoped, that in the fullness of time, the party would lead Russia and the world to Communism.

Glossary

1905 Revolution A series of events during 1905 in Russia which threatened to overthrow the Tsar. The 1905 Revolution did not destroy Tsarism, but it did lead to some reforms.

Abdication When a monarch steps down from their position as king or queen.

Agents provocateurs Police spies that pose as members of illegal organisations and encourage their members to break the law.

Anarchism A political movement dedicated to overthrowing capitalism and the state.

Autonomy Self-government.

Baltic states Three countries with coastlines on the Baltic Sea: Estonia, Latvia and Lithuania.

Bicameral A parliament that has two chambers or houses, which must work together to make law.

Black Hundreds A violent extremist nationalist group that supported Tsarism.

Bolshevik Central Committee Leading committee of the Bolshevik Party.

Bolsheviks A faction of the Russian Social Democratic Party, led by Lenin.

Bourgeoisie The term used by Karl Marx to describe the middle class.

Cabinet The most senior committee in government.

Cheka The political police force created by Lenin.

Civil society Organisations such as religious groups, clubs and businesses which are not part of the state.

Civil war A war between different groups within a nation.

Communism The belief that private ownership should be abolished, and all work and property should be shared by the community. In the twentieth century it became a political movement based upon the ideas and writings of Karl Marx.

Constituent Assembly An elected body which was supposed to design a constitution for Russia after the Tsar was deposed. The Assembly met once and was then dissolved by force by Lenin's revolutionary government.

Constitutional checks Legal measures which stop the government acting in a dictatorial way.

Constitutional government A government that has to act in a way which reflects the law.

Constitutional monarchy A monarch whose power is constrained by the constitution.

Constitutional reform Changes to the fundamental laws of a country.

Consultative An organisation which seeks or offers advice. Significantly, a government may ignore the advice offered.

Corruption An abuse of power, in which a government or government official uses their power inappropriately.

Cossacks A people group who originate from southern Russia. They were famous for their horse skills and fighting abilities. In return for control over their own land they served in the Russian military. The Tsars often used them to suppress rebellions across Russia.

Counter-revolutionaries People or groups who want to return to the way things were before the revolution.

Czech Legion During the First World War, Czechs had been conscripted to the Austro-Hungarian army and thousands had been taken prisoner. The Provisional Government promised to free the Czechs to fight against Germany and Austria–Hungary. The agreement collapsed when Lenin signed the Treaty of Brest-Litovsk. The Czechs rebelled and fought against the Communists.

De facto A Latin term meaning 'according to the facts'. It is often contrasted with **de jure** meaning 'according to the law'.

Enfranchised Given the right to vote, or to have some say, in government.

Faction A group of people within a political party, who share a common set of beliefs and who are in opposition to the leadership of the party.

Freedom of assembly The right to meet with others and organise politically or socially.

Freedom of conscience The right to practise any religion or no religion.

Greens This group fought against the Reds and the Whites during the Civil War. They drew support from peasants and their policies focused on redistributing land to the peasants.

Hyperinflation An economic situation in which inflation increases dramatically, usually for a sustained period.

Idealists   People who advocate policies that are morally or ethically right, rather than policies believed to be practical.

Indirect elections   Elections which select the people responsible for selecting the people who hold power. They are contrasted with direct elections in which the electorate selects the people who hold power.

Justices of the peace   Judges who administered law in Russia's villages after the 1905 Revolution.

Kadets   A radical liberal group, which emerged from the 1905 Revolution. They demanded further constitutional reforms from the Tsar.

Kronstadt naval base   This was a large naval base located outside Petrograd. In 1917, the sailors of Petrograd had turned against the Tsar and the Provisional Government. They also posed a threat to Lenin and the Communists in 1921.

Land reform   The process of redistributing land, usually from large landowners to poor peasants.

Legislative   Law making.

Liberal   People, ideas or organisations that believe in individual rights.

Liberal democratic regime   A society in which people elect their government and in which individual rights are respected.

'Little Father'   A nickname for the Tsar, implying that he was caring and similar to God, who was referred to as a father.

Martial law   A situation in which ordinary people are placed under the control of the military.

Marxist ideology   Ideas inspired by Karl Marx.

Mensheviks   A faction of the Russian Social Democratic Party which disagreed with Lenin's interpretation of revolutionary politics. The majority of Mensheviks opposed the October Revolution. The party continued until the early 1920s when it was finally outlawed.

Military Revolutionary Committee   Leadership of armed forces loyal to the Petrograd Soviet, which included the Red Guard.

Mixed economy   An economy in which the state and private enterprise both play a significant role.

Nationalist   A person or a group who believes that their nation should govern itself. Nationalists can also believe that their nation has a special character which gives it the right to rule other nations.

Nihilism   A political movement which rejected the authority of the church, the government and the aristocracy. Nihilists wanted to liberate Russia's peasants and were willing to use violence in order to achieve their goals.

Octoberists   Name given to those Russian politicians who had supported the introduction of the October Manifesto after the 1905 Russian Revolution.

Okhrana   The Tsar's secret police.

Open letter   A letter which is published in the press, and therefore can be read by the public as well as the person it is addressed to.

Orthodox   A type of Christianity that originated in Eastern Europe, Greece and Russia.

Pale of Jewish Settlement   A western region of Imperial Russia, in which Russian Jews were allowed to live permanently.

Pogroms   Organised violence, typically against Jews in parts of the Russian Empire in the nineteenth and twentieth centuries.

Politburo   Consisted of approximately nine Communists who met every week to make key political and economic decisions. During the Civil War they became even more significant than the Sovnarkom.

Political prisoners   People who are imprisoned for political reasons, rather than for committing crimes.

Proletariat   Term used by Karl Marx to describe the industrial working classes.

Promulgated   The point at which a law is published and put into effect.

Proselytise   Attempt to convert people to a religion.

Provisional Government   The government that ruled the Russian Empire on a temporary basis after the fall of the Tsar. The Provisional Government was deposed by Lenin's October Revolution.

Ratify   To agree something formally.

Reactionary   A person, group, or policy which is highly conservative.

Real terms   Increases or decreases in funding which take inflation into account.

Red Guards   Numbered approximately 100,000 men, they were the elite fighting force of the Bolsheviks.

Reds   Name given to the Communists fighting during the Civil War.

Reformist   A person, group or policy which tries to achieve change through peaceful and legal methods.

Requisitioned   Goods which are formally demanded by the government for important purposes.

Reservists   Troops who are held in reserve.

Russian Empire   A group of countries controlled by the Tsar, one of the biggest Empires in the world in the nineteenth century.

Russification The process by which Russian culture and language was forced upon different ethnic groups across the Russian Empire.

Self-determination The principle that each national people group should decide their own destiny.

Senate A senior committee which advised the Tsar.

Separate peace A proposed peace treaty between Russia, Germany and Austro-Hungary, which did not include the British, French or other warring nations.

Socialist A person, political party or policy that aims to ensure that working people, rather than property owners, benefit fully from industrialisation.

Sovnarkom The most powerful body within the Bolshevik government.

State Council A senior committee which advised the Tsar.

State of emergency A declaration from the government that gives government ministers special powers for a temporary period in order to deal with a crisis.

Subjects People ruled over by a monarch or emperor. Unlike citizens, subjects have no rights and play no role in government.

Tax in kind A tax in which producers pay the government a proportion of what they make, rather than paying in money.

Temporary Regulations Laws introduced in 1883 which gave the Okhrana widespread powers to oppress opposition.

Troudoviks A group of moderate socialists who stood for election to the Dumas.

Universal suffrage Voting rights for all adults.

Vesenkha The organisation within Lenin's government which controlled the economy.

War Communism A series of economic policies introduced by the Communists in order to win the Civil War.

Whites Fought against the Reds during the Civil War and consisted of different groups, such as ex-supporters of the Tsar and the Provisional Government. This group was also supported by foreign troops.

Winter Palace The Tsar's residence in St Petersburg. It became the centre of the Provisional Government in 1917.

Zemgor The union of zemstvos and towns, it co-ordinated voluntary aid for Russian soldiers during the First World War.

Zemstvo Hussars Military units organised by Zemgor during the Civil War.

Key figures

Viktor Chernov (1873–1952) A revolutionary, intellectual and politician. Chernov was leader of the Socialist Revolutionaries. He was elected to the Second Duma, and later served as Minister for Agriculture in the Provisional Government. After the Bolshevik seizure of power Chernov formed an alternative government in Samara. Chernov's government was crushed during the Civil War.

Felix Dzerzhinsky (1877–1926) Born into an aristocratic family, Dzerzhinsky considered becoming a Catholic priest, before becoming a Marxist. He was a member of several revolutionary organisations before joining the Bolsheviks in 1917. From 1917 until his death he was head of the Communist political police.

Father Gapon Father Gapon played the leading role in organising the march to the Winter Palace. He also wrote the petition that the marchers intended to deliver to the Tsar. Gapon was a radical Orthodox priest who was sincerely concerned with improving the lives of the poor. Prior to the march Gapon organised the Assembly of Factory and Mill Workers of St Petersburg. The organisation quickly spread throughout the city. By 1905 it had 8,000 members. Initially, Gapon's organisation had been a 'Police Union', established as part of Zubatov's 'Police Socialism' initiative (see page 8). However, by 1905 the Okhrana had abandoned 'Police Socialism' and Gapon was working on his own initiative.

Alexander Kerensky (1881–1970) A lawyer and politician, who played a key role in the Provisional Government. Kerensky was a member of the Fourth Duma. He also worked as a radical lawyer defending revolutionaries against the Russian state. He was Justice Minister, the Minister for War and finally head of the Provisional Government.

Lavr Kornilov (1870–1918)   A senior military leader in the Russia Imperial Army, Kornilov was appointed commander-in-chief in 1917. Kornilov's failed coup against the Provisional Government strengthened the Bolsheviks. He was killed fighting Bolshevik forces in April 1918.

Vladimir Lenin (1870–1924)   A Marxist, revolutionary, journalist and intellectual. He became leader of the Bolsheviks after they split from the Social Democratic Party in 1903. His views on Marxism were highly influential in Russia.

Prince Lvov (1861–1925)   An aristocrat and politician, he was the first leader of the Provisional Government that replaced the Tsar in 1917. Lvov organised relief work during the Russo-Japanese War, and was leader of the Union of Zemstvos during the First World War. He was also a member of the Duma.

Karl Marx (1818–83)   A German philosopher, revolutionary and journalist. His ideas on class and revolution were extremely influential on Russian intellectuals. Lenin and his followers considered themselves Marxists.

Pavel Milyukov (1859–1943)   A liberal politician, one of the founders of the League of Liberation in 1903. Following the 1905 Revolution he became the leader of the Kadets. He also became the Foreign Minister within the Provisional Government in 1917. He opposed the autocratic power of the Tsar.

Nicholas II (1868–1918)   Nicholas Romanov, Russia's last Tsar. Nicholas II was a highly conservative and deeply religious leader.

Grigori Rasputin (1869–1916)   A mystical holy man, one of a number of religious influences on the Tsar. Nicholas II believed that Rasputin had the power to heal, and heard the voice of God. Rasputin had a reputation as a drunk and a womaniser. Nonetheless, he was highly charismatic and had many followers.

Joseph Stalin (1878–1953)   Born into a poor Georgian family, Stalin was educated in a church school. He joined the Bolsheviks in 1903 and was involved in revolutionary activity from the outset. Stalin was forced into exile by the Okhrana on a number of occasions. He was a member of Lenin's first Politburo and played a major role in government under Lenin, before becoming leader of the Soviet Union after Lenin's death.

Pyotr Stolypin (1862–1911)   Stolypin was one of the Tsar's most trusted ministers in the years after the 1905 Revolution. His policies of repression and reform helped stabilise Tsarism in the years after 1905. The Tsar lost faith in Stolypin around 1910, partly because Stolypin wanted to ban Rasputin from seeing the Tsar in St Petersburg. Stolypin was assassinated in 1911 by a revolutionary who also worked as an informant for the Okhrana.

Pyotr Struve (1870–1944)   A liberal politician, one of the founders of the League of Liberation in 1903. Following the 1905 Revolution he became the leader of the Kadets. He supported the Whites during the Civil War.

Leon Trotsky (1879–1940)   A Marxist, revolutionary, journalist and intellectual. He came to fame as revolutionary leader of the St Petersburg Soviet in 1905. For many years he was engaged in public disputes with Lenin. However, he joined the Bolsheviks in 1917 and played a leading role in Lenin's government. His heroic reputation was enhanced by his leadership of the Red Army during the Civil War.

Sergei Witte (1849–1915)   One of the Tsar's most trusted ministers and advisers. Witte played a key role promoting industrialisation. As Russia's prime minister he advised the Tsar to compromise with liberals during the 1905 Revolution. His influence led to the publication of the October Manifesto.

Answers

1: The rule of Nicholas II, 1894–1905

Page 7, Identify the concept

1 'The fundamental problems with autocracy were the main reason for the collapse of Tsarism in the period 1894–1917.' How far do you agree with this statement? *cause*
2 How far did Tsarist rule change in the period 1894–1905? **AS** *change/continuity*
3 How accurate is it to say that Nicholas II's rule was fundamentally unstable in the years 1894–1905? *change/continuity*
4 How far do you agree that Russification was responsible for the political stability of Russia in the years 1894–1904? **AS** *cause*
5 How far was political unrest the most important consequence of Nicholas II's autocratic rule in the period 1894–1905? *consequence*
6 'Nicholas II's policies fundamentally undermined autocratic rule in the period 1894–1914.' How far do you agree with this view? *cause*

Page 19, Identify the concept

1 'Opposition to Tsarism had little impact on Tsarist rule in the period prior to the 1905 Revolution.' How far do you agree with this statement? *consequence*
2 How accurate is it to say that the 1905 Revolution was a turning point in Nicholas II's reign, 1894 and 1914? *change/continuity*
3 Were Russia's growing economic problems the main reason for the outbreak of the Revolution in January 1905? Explain your answer. **AS** *cause*
4 'Nicholas II's power was fundamentally weakened by the 1905 Revolution.' How far do you agree with this statement? *change/continuity*
5 How accurate is it to say that Nicholas II's reactionary policies weakened the government of Russia in the years 1894–1905? *change/continuity*
6 How significant was the work of the Okhrana for the stability of Tsarism in the years 1894–1904? **AS** *significance*

Page 19, The flaw in the argument

The argument claims that the demand made by liberals had a significant impact on Tsarist rule. However, making demands does not necessarily make a difference.

Page 21, Identify key terms

'The <u>essential features of autocracy</u> survived the 1905 Revolution.' How far do you agree with this statement?

2: The end of Romanov rule, 1906–17

Page 29, Identify the concept

1 How significant were the Fundamental Laws in the survival of the Tsar's autocracy in the years 1906–14? *significance*
2 How far was the 1905 Revolution a turning point in Tsarist government, in the period 1894–1914? *change/continuity*
3 How far did the Fundamental Laws of 1906 reassert the essential features of Tsarist autocracy? *change/ continuity* or *similarity/difference*
4 To what extent did the Fundamental Laws achieve Nicholas II's aims in the period 1906–14? **AS** *consequence*
5 Was the 1905 Revolution the main reason for the introduction of the Fundamental Laws in April 1906? **AS** *cause*

Page 31, Write the question – suggested

1 How far could the historian make use of Sources 1 and 2 together to investigate the nature of Stolypin's government in the period 1906–11?
2 Why is Source 1 valuable to the historian for an enquiry into the effectiveness of Stolypin's government in the period 1906–11?

Page 33, Identify key terms

'Between 1906 and 1914 the Tsar's government was <u>wholly reactionary</u>.' How far do you agree with this statement?

Page 37, Develop the detail – suggested

The military was one aspect of Russia that was only partially modernised in the years 1906–14. There were some attempts to modernise the army such as a new plan in 1908, which set out a ten-year programme to modernise the army, including the introduction of military aircraft.

However, the plan did not tackle some of the long-standing problems, such as incompetent generals, the lack of education among Russian soldiers, who were the least educated in Europe, and the underdeveloped state of Russian industry. Also by 1914 the plan had not fully taken effect. Finally, aspects of the plan were ineffective as they did not address Russia's real defence needs. Indeed, the Tsar authorised a massive programme of naval expansion in 1907 which was expensive and useless as Russia faced no major naval threats. Therefore, the Russian military was only partially modernised as the reforms that were introduced did not prepare Russia to fight a truly modern war in 1914.

Page 37, You're the examiner

Level 3 – this answer is descriptive, and does truly not evaluate the extent of modernisation.

Page 39, Spot the inference

- The Duma was elected by the Russian people. *X*
- The government's attitude to the Zemgor was inexplicable. The Zemgor did some good work, but spent too much money, and Prince Lvov would have been made to pay for his anarchist principles if the revolution had not happened. *P*
- The Zemgor was better funded than official government departments. *I*
- The author of Source 1 believed that the government had a contradictory attitude to the Zemgor, as it both gave the Zemgor money and distrusted it. *P*
- The author of Source 1 believed that the Zemgor had revolutionary intentions prior to the February Revolution. *X*

3: The Provisional Government and its opponents, February-October 1917

Page 47, Spot the mistake

The answer is focused and detailed, but it does not conclude with an analytical link back to the question.

Page 57, Develop the detail

Kerensky's political failings were clearly one reason for the downfall of the Provisional Government by October 1917. Kerensky was responsible for the June Offensive, an important military defeat. This led to the July Days, an uprising that almost overthrew the Provisional Government. Kerensky also undermined the government by introducing repressive measures, such as press censorship and military courts which punished deserters and Bolsheviks. His appointment of a new army leader also backfired. The conservative General Lavr Kornilov attempted to overthrow the government in a coup in August 1917. Clearly, Kerensky's political failings

were one reason for the downfall of the Provisional Government because his decisions tended to weaken support for the government.

Page 59, Write the question

1 How far could the historian make use of Sources 1 and 2 together to investigate the extent of popular support for the Military Revolutionary Committee in October 1917?

2 How much weight do you give the evidence of Source 2 for an enquiry into the extent of popular support for the Military Revolutionary Committee in October 1917?

4: Defending the Bolshevik revolution, October 1917-24

Page 69, Identify an argument

The second paragraph includes an argument.

Page 71, Spot the inference

- The Constituent Assembly was elected by the Russian people. *X*
- The writers of Source 1 believe that Sovnarkom was pursuing counter-revolutionary policies. *I*
- The writers of Source 1 do not believe that all Bolsheviks are counter-revolutionaries. *I*
- The Left SRs believe that the Treaty of Brest-Litovsk was forced on Russia by the Germans. *X*
- The writers of Source 1 believe the Left SRs should start a terrorist campaign against Sovnarkom, to save the values of the Russian Revolution. *P*
- The writers of Source 1 believe that terrorist action will inspire the workers and peasants to rise up against the government. *P*

The Left SRs want to assassinate Lenin. *X*

Page 77, You're the examiner

Level 3. It is focused and contains some accurate detail, but it does not contain an analytical link back to the question.

Page 79, Write the question

1 How far could the historian make use of Sources 1 and 2 together to investigate the extent of popular support for Lenin's government in the six months after the October Revolution?

2 Why is Source 1 valuable to the historian for an enquiry into Lenin's approach to government in the first months following the October Revolution?

Mark scheme

AO1 mark scheme

- Analytical focus
- Accurate detail
- Supported judgement
- Argument and structure

AS Marks		A-level Marks
1–4	**Level 1** • Simplistic, limited focus • Limited detail, limited accuracy • No judgement or asserted judgement • Limited organisation, no argument	1–3
5–10	**Level 2** • Descriptive, implicit focus • Limited detail, mostly accurate • Judgement with limited support • Basic organisation, limited argument	4–7
11–16	**Level 3** • Some analysis, clear focus (maybe descriptive in places) • Some detail, mostly accurate • Judgement with some support, based on implicit criteria • Some organisation, the argument is broadly clear	11–16
17–20	**Level 4** • Clear analysis, clear focus (maybe uneven) • Sufficient detail, mostly accurate • Judgement with some support, based on valid criteria • Generally well organised, logical argument (may lack precision)	13–16
	Level 5 • Sustained analysis, clear focus • Sufficient accurate detail, fully answers the question • Judgement with full support, based on valid criteria (considers relative significance) • Well organised, logical argument communicated with precision	17–20

AO2 mark scheme – AS

- Source analysis
- Detail from context
- Evaluation of source material

AS (a) Marks		AS (b) Marks
1–2	**Level 1** • Surface level comprehension of the source demonstrated through quoting and paraphrasing • Some relevant knowledge, not linked to the source • Limited evaluation of source material in relation to the enquiry, with simplistic support	1–2
3–5	**Level 2** • Limited understanding of the source demonstrated through selection and summarising • Some relevant knowledge, expands or confirms evidence from the source (or challenges source material in Part b) • Evaluates the source material in relation to the enquiry, but with limited support	3–5

AS (a) Marks		AS (b) Marks
6–8	**Level 3** ● Understanding of the source demonstrated through selection, summarising and valid inferences ● Relevant knowledge, explains and expands on the source, and supports valid inferences (or challenges source material in Part b) ● Evaluates the source material in relation to the enquiry, by considering valid criteria such as the nature and origin of the source	6–9
	Level 4 ● Analyses the source material demonstrated through an interrogation of the source to make reasoned inferences. Distinctions may be made between information and claim or opinion ● Relevant knowledge, discusses strengths and limitations of the source. Begins to consider the values and assumptions of the society from which the source is taken when interpreting the source ● Evaluates the source material in relation to the enquiry, by considering valid criteria to weigh the evidence. Some evaluation may lack support	10–12

AO2 mark scheme – A-level

- Source analysis
- Detail from context
- Evaluation of source material

	A-level Marks
Level 1 ● Surface level comprehension of the sources demonstrated through quoting and paraphrasing ● Some relevant knowledge, not linked to the sources ● Limited evaluation of source material in relation to the enquiry, with simplistic support	1–3
Level 2 ● Some understanding of the sources demonstrated through summarising and making undeveloped inferences ● Some relevant knowledge, expands, confirms or challenges evidence from the sources ● Evaluates the source material in relation to the enquiry, but with limited or questionable support	4–7
Level 3 ● Understanding of the sources demonstrated through selection, summarising and valid inferences ● Relevant knowledge, explains and expands on the sources, and supports or challenges valid inferences ● Evaluates the source material in relation to the enquiry, by considering valid criteria such as the nature and origin of the source	8–12
Level 4 ● Analyses the sources demonstrated through an interrogation of the source to make reasoned inferences. Distinctions may be made between information and claim or opinion. Treatment of the sources may be uneven ● Relevant knowledge, discusses strengths and limitations of the source. Begins to consider the values and assumptions of the society from which the source is taken when interpreting the sources ● Evaluates the source material in relation to the enquiry, by considering valid criteria to weigh the evidence. Some evaluation may lack support	13–16
Level 5 ● Analyses the sources demonstrated through a confident and discriminating interrogation of the source to make reasoned inferences. Distinctions may be made between information and claim or opinion ● Relevant knowledge, discusses strengths and limitations of the source. Considers the values and assumptions of the society from which the source is taken when interpreting the sources ● Evaluates the source material in relation to the enquiry, by considering valid criteria to weigh the evidence. Where appropriate, distinguishes between the degrees of certainty with which aspects of the sources can be used as the basis for claims	17–20